Debating Empire

Edited by
GOPAL BALAKRISHNAN

with contributions by

Stanley Aronowitz, Giovanni Arrighi, Timothy Brennan,
Malcolm Bull, Alex Callinicos, Sam Gindin, Tom Mertes,
Leo Panitch, Michael Rustin, Sanjay Seth, Charles Tilly
and Ellen Meiksins Wood

VERSO
London • New York

First published by Verso 2003
© in the collection Verso 2003
All rights reserved

The moral rights of the authors have been asserted

1 3 5 7 9 10 8 6 4 2

Verso
UK: 6 Meard Street, London W1F 0EG
USA: 180 Varick Street, New York, NY 10014–4606
www.versobooks.com

Verso is the imprint of New Left Books

ISBN 1–85984–530–4
ISBN 1–85984–452–9 (pbk)

British Library Cataloguing in Publication Data
A catalogue record for this book is available from the British Library

Library of Congress Cataloging-in-Publication Data
Debating empire / edited by Gopal Balakrishnan; with contributions by Stanley Aronowitz
. . . [et al.].
    p. cm.
Includes index.
ISBN 1-85984-530-4 (cloth) – ISBN 1-85984-452-9 (pbk)
1. Socialism. 2. New Left. 3. Capitalism. 4. Globalization. 5. International economic
relations. 6. Political science–Philosophy. I. Balakrishnan, Gopal. II. Aronowitz, Stanley.

HX44.5.D43 2003
335–dc21

                                                                              2003053521

Typeset in 10/12.5pt Baskerville by SetSystems Ltd, Saffron Walden, Essex
Printed & bound in UK by Clowes

Debating Empire

Contents

Introduction

Gopal Balakrishnan

No word resonates more strongly today than 'Empire', the title of a literary sensation that has given a name to an enigmatic totality of money, power and culture. The reception of this co-authored manifesto already forms an episode of contemporary intellectual history: a work of ornate erudition, professing communist allegiances, becoming a bestseller in an atmosphere of improbable media fanfare. Since its publication in 2000, it has a attracted a steady stream of reviews, a cross-section of which appear in this reader. *Debating Empire* is a collection of radical responses to Michael Hardt and Antonio Negri's bold, synoptic vision of the volatile landscapes of the world system. Such works are provisional illuminations of a historical process that appears to unfold in a narrative of decades. It is important to keep in mind, then, that the contributors to this reader are responding to a text that was written between the first Gulf War and the Kosovo intervention, at a time when the world capitalist system seemed 'miraculously healthy and robust', and the relationship between America and the top tier of Eurasian powers more relaxed. The ongoing relevance of *Empire* as an interventionist text will depend on the strength of its responses to the sharpest turns of events and criticisms.

Empire has set the stage for a critique of the master rhetorics of globalization, resuming the work of a Marxist tradition from an earlier strategic conjuncture. Prior to its publication, diagnoses from the left seemed to offer either a bleak scan of the historic bottom line, or – alternately – consolation prizes. At best, the alternative to surrender or self-delusion seemed to be a combative but clear-eyed pessimism, orienting the mind for a Long March against the new scheme of things. In this atmosphere, the recent appearance of *Empire* has represented a spectacular break. Michael Hardt and Antonio Negri defiantly overturn the verdict that the last two decades were a time of punitive defeats for the left. After years of living in French exile, Negri returned to serve the sentence he received in Italy in the early 1980s, during the crack down on the far left, initially writing as an inmate from the Rebibbia Prison in Rome, where once Gramsci was held under fascism. But the work he and Hardt have written owes very little to the precedent of the *Prison Notebooks*. Few messages could be further from that harsh strategic reckoning than the argument of *Empire*. Its burden is that, appearances to the contrary, we live in a springtime of peoples, a world overflowing with insurgent energies. In a period where others merely cast about for silver linings, Hardt and Negri announce a golden age.

Empire develops its rousing theme in an attractive variety of registers. The collaboration between American literary theorist and Italian political philosopher has produced a strange and graceful work, of rare imaginative drive and richness of intellectual reference. Theoretically, and to some extent architectonically, Hardt and Negri situate themselves in the line of Deleuze and Guattari's *Thousand Plateaux*. Their work freely crosses disciplinary boundaries, venturing reflections on law, culture, politics, economics with a repertoire of concepts drawing on sources ranging from the canon of European classical philosophy to the findings of contemporary American social science and cultural studies, not to speak of sidelights from Celine or Kafka, Herman Melville or Robert Musil. However counter-intuitive its conclusions, *Empire* is in its own terms a work of visionary intensity.

The formal construction of this text raises a series of problems addressed by Timothy Brennan, whose contribution offers a trenchant critique of its method of composing illustrious intellectual lineages. Brennan sceptically evaluates Hardt and Negri's conception of theory as *assemblage* – an assortment of motifs plucked from disparate classical works, arranged into dazzling, yet intellectually fragile, bouquets. In Nietzschean terms, this is historical consciousness in an antiquarian, as opposed to critical, mode. *Empire* thematizes the horizons of an emerging Italian ideological formation that sanctions the declension of politics to a mere structure of feeling – revolutionary emoting, as it were. In this fashion the harsh realities of modern capitalism and state power are refracted into hazy, enabling figures. Empire is ultimately a Sorelian myth of empowerment, offering consolation to oppositional desire, in place of a sober political realism.

The authors of *Empire* would claim that every explosive expansion of the *known world* from the early modern conquest of the New World to the New Times of globalization has sparked outpourings of utopian desire that have scrambled inherited intellectual schemas, offering new possibilities of association and action. Seen in this light, their elective genealogies are an attempt to trace the shimmering arc of human agency back to the inaugural moment of modernity – the European Renaissance. Hardt and Negri define modernity as an epochal crisis brought on by the simultaneously liberating and enslaving expansion of the European world, progressively shattering all forms of life sanctioned by transcendent authority. Brecht's Galileo captures the paradigmatic moment in the historical narrative of *Empire*: a Renaissance outbreak of the will to truth and power, followed by the restoration of a mortally threatened ancien regime. During the subsequent volatile centuries of politico-intellectual civil war, the ominous figure of the modern state crystallized to contain the challenge of this radical secularization, neutralizing it through a metaphysics of indivisible sovereignty. The contemporary era of globalization is celebrated in *Empire* as the historic terminus of this previously immutable political form.

Although Hardt and Negri open their case by arguing that nation-state-based systems of power are rapidly unravelling in the force-fields of world capitalism, globalization cannot be understood as a simple process of de-regulating markets. Far from withering away, regulations today proliferate and interlock to form an acephelous supranational order. The term 'Empire', as they use it, refers not to a system in which tribute flows from peripheries to great capital cities, but to a more Foucauldian figure – a diffuse, anonymous network of all-englobing power. Hardt and Negri claim that the sinews of this phantasmic polity – its flows of people, information, and wealth – are simply too unruly to be monitored from metropolitan control centres. Their account of its origins adds a few striking nuances to a now familiar

story. An older statist world of ruling class and proletariat, of
dominant core and subject periphery, is breaking down, and in
its place a less dichotomous and more intricate pattern of inequality is emerging. 'Empire' could be described as the planetary
gestalt of these flows and hierarchies.

The historical sociologist Giovanni Arrighi maintains that there
is no evidence for the claim that the awesome material gap
between the affluent core and dependent peripheries of world
capitalism dating from the colonial era is now closing. In a concise
brief, Charles Tilly goes further, dismissing *Empire* as a speculative
caricature of the real world of power, money and mobility. Its
central claims, he insists, are either unfalsifiable or false.

Indeed it is often hard to separate and test individual theses of
this work, apart from the imposing claim of the whole. Hardt and
Negri maintain that the logic of this volatile totality evades and
transgresses all the inherited divisions of political thought: state
and society, war and peace, control and freedom, as well as core
and periphery; even the distinction between systemic and anti-
systemic agency is blurred beyond recognition. The advent of this
Empire is thus not merely a momentous episode in world history,
it is an event of considerable ontological importance, heralded
here in the voice of impassioned prophecy.

The rupture in the history of capitalism that the authors
announce invites inevitable comparisons to Marxist analyses from
the beginning of the last century – most notably Lenin's attempt
to compose 'a general picture of the world capitalist system in its
international relationships at the beginning of the 20th century –
on the eve of the imperialist world war'. Lenin's pamphlet portrayed a process of market competition generating monopolies
controlled by banks, locked into a frenzied struggle to secure
investment opportunities in foreign raw materials, railways and
public debt, eventually escalating into struggles for exclusive
spheres of influence and inevitable wars for the redivision of the
most lucrative spheres.

Lenin portrayed imperialism as the *latest* phase of capitalism,
beyond which there could be others, unless the entire system
were overturned in a world revolution. According to Hardt and
Negri, the historic result of the failure of the latter enterprise is
Empire – the *last* instance of a successful restructuring of capitalism under the impact of war and rebellion. They insist that a

cyclical account of a series of eras of capitalism cannot subsume the unprecedented geopolitical, economic and cultural logics of Empire. Against this claim, Arrighi defends his own alternative account of the novelty of the long American century and considers the possible geometry of global political economies beyond it. It is generally thought that if the contemporary world system can be described as an empire, it is because of the overwhelming concentration of financial, diplomatic and military power in American hands. The overlords of Washington and New York themselves no longer shy away from the word 'imperialism' as an apt description of their planetary agendas. Hardt and Negri, however, reject any idea that the United States can be described as an imperialist power. For Empire in the upper-case from, with no definite article, excludes any state-based imperialism. But it could be argued that the decline of the nation-state – the deterioration of its extractive, planning and war-making capacities – is simply the harvest of resurgent American power seeking to restructure the rules of world market competition, international law, and warfare to lock in its position for the coming century. One state, at least, is not withering away in the era of globalization.

But it would be implausible to suggest that the authors of Empire have simply spun out a new version of a shop-worn globalization rhetoric. The latter characteristically euphemizes the realities of the world market with the soft-focus notion of civil society. Hardt and Negri, by contrast, coolly dismiss the claim that even the most blameless NGOs are agencies of a global civil society pitted against the established powers. Rather they can be compared to the Dominicans and Jesuits of late feudal society, functioning as 'the charitable campaigns and mendicant orders of Empire'. Media-staged crusades by Amnesty International or Médecins sans Frontières play an essential role in mobilizing public opinion behind humanitarian interventionism. It is no surprise that Hardt and Negri's critique of interventionist jargon relies heavily on the writings of Carl Schmitt.

> The traditional concept of just war involves the banalization of war and the celebration of it as an ethical instrument, both of which were ideas that modern political thought and the international community of nation-states resolutely refused. These two traditional characteristics

have reappeared in our postmodern world . . . Today the enemy, just like war itself, comes to be at once banalized (reduced to an object of routine police suppression) and absolutized (as the Enemy, an absolute threat to the ethical order).

One of the paradoxes of Empire is that it sets into motion a reversal of the process of secularization that defined the modern era. It is a world order in perpetual hot pursuit of absolute enemies: terrorists, Islamic fundamentalists and rogue nationalist regimes are the targets of its crusading fury. Empire is, in legal terms, engulfed in a 'permanent state of emergency and exception justified by the appeal to essential values'. Although powerful and succinct, this formulation is difficult to reconcile with Hardt and Negri's insistence that Empire is a coherent constitutional structure, a self-enclosed legal system of the sort imagined by Hans Kelsen. A constitution engulfed in a permanent state of exception cannot form a self-enclosed legal system, and is, in fact, only nominally a juridical order. The ambiguities of *Empire* on this point are symptomatic: many of the institutions that initially loomed large at the end of the Cold War and appeared to form the architecture of a New World order under Washington oversight – most importantly the United Nations and NATO – are faltering under the hammer blows of American power.

According to Ellen Wood, *Empire*'s globalization paradigm cannot account for the indispensable role of territorially organized state power in the reproduction of capitalist social relations. The sovereign monopoly of domestic violence is simultaneously inserted in an anarchic interstate system that embraces and holds the world market in place. Although the anarchy of this geopolitical field has been contained for half a century by the ultimate sovereignty of the American state, the latter is now playing this role in an increasingly destabilizing fashion.

But Hardt and Negri do not always seem to accept the claim that Empire has to be seen as the manifestation of the unfolding logic of capital. For the political order they portray has a universal mission of pacification comparable to those Empires of the past that strove to embrace the known world. Virgil is cited to convey the sheer magnitude of the change: 'The final age that the oracle foretold has arrived; the great order of the centuries is born again.' While Hardt and Negri discern a clean break between this system and the state-based colonialisms that preceded it, they place great stock in more ancient genealogies of this postmodern Empire. Those who want to understand the new universe should look to the writings of Polybius who sought to explain to stupefied contemporaries how it was that Rome had risen to become master of the Mediterranean world. Polybius held that Rome had transcended the unstable cycles of the classical polis, because its constitution mixed monarchy, aristocracy and democracy in proportions that checked the degenerative potential inherent in any unalloyed form of government. Hardt and Negri argue that the new world order can be envisaged as an analogous structure, in which US nuclear supremacy represents the monarchical principle, the economic wealth of the G8 and transnational corporations the aristocratic principle, and the internet the democratic principle – Bomb, Money and Ether composing the contemporary version of the constitution of the Roman Republic, on the morrow of its defeat of Carthage. But if this use of Polybius suggests an Empire at the threshold of centuries of ascendancy, other classical allusions – Montesquieu or Gibbon – suggest simply eclipse or decline: tropes not just of universal order, but of decadence, transvaluation and crumbling *limes*. In this register, Hardt and Negri liken potential revolutionaries of today to Christians of the later Roman Empire, witnessing the inexorable hollowing out of the terrestrial order of things and the beginnings of a new, rejuvenating era of barbarian migrations. Parallels with the Ancient World, central to the rhetorical strategy of *Empire*, oscillate between alternative meanings: do they point to the rising or the falling fortunes of global capitalism?

Overall, the book suggests the latter. Empire, its authors insist, did not emerge out of the defeat of systemic challenges to capital. On the contrary, its existence stands as a resounding, if paradoxical, testimony to the heroic mass struggles that shattered the Eurocentric old regime of national states and colonialism. But the project of Third World revolutionary nationalism – although driven by emulation of the metropolitan core – simultaneously presupposed an anti-systemic exit option from the world market. As a generalization, it could be said that the accelerated erosion of the peasantry as an object of modernization signals the end of an era of subaltern nationalisms, as the annexation of the space outside the world market moves to completion.

But in sharp contrast to the theorists of a post-colonial condition, who also challenge national narratives of self-determination, the authors of *Empire* maintain that the homogenizing fictions of sovereign nationhood cannot be countered with a politics of cultural difference. For mere heteroglossia or hybridization offer no alternative: the ideology of Empire has become a supple, multicultural aesthetic that de-activates the revolutionary possibilities of globalization. Far from being oppositional, academic enthusiasts for diversity articulate the inclusive logic of a spontaneous order that no longer depends upon a metaphysics of natural difference and hierarchy. Dissenting from this view, Sanjay Seth argues that this rejection of the post-colonial critique of Eurocentrism threatens to efface the anti-systemic agencies at the cultural margins of Empire.

Running through the work is the fervent belief that contemporary capitalism, although seemingly impervious to anti-systemic challenge, is in fact vulnerable at all points to riot and rebellion. The increasing importance of immaterial, intellectual labour in high-value-added sectors of the economy is shaping a collective labourer with heightened powers of subversion. But in order to assess the potential combativity of this multifarious proletariat, Leo Panitch and Sam Gindich insist that a sharper picture is needed of competition-driven innovations in finance, technology and political regulation that are reshaping the world of labour. Although warmly congratulating the revolutionary spirit of the work, both suggest that *Empire*'s rousing vision of the new American worker cannot point the way out for those imprisoned by the American dream.

Disregarding the formidable atomizing power of capital at work across the entire range of working class experience, *Empire* speaks of an ineradicable plebeian desire for emancipation stoked by the increasingly apparent malleability of all social relationships and the permeability of all borders. The global multitude, embracing all those who work, or are just poor, from computer scientists in Palo Alto to slum-dwellers in São Paulo, forms a class that, in its very quotidian mode of existence, is somehow revolutionary.

What historic experience lies behind these counter-intuitive assertions? Around the mid-seventies Negri came to the conclusion that the industrial working class was no longer an agent of social revolution. Out of a mounting ultra-left frustration in the face of deadlocked class struggles, he drew an innovative re-reading of Marx's *Grundrisse* that dissolved any hard proletarian core into a broader pool of the dispossesed and disaffected. The latter, he contended, were just as essential to the reproduction of capital, and more prone to volatile upsurges. His prediction that a new social worker was taking shape, although more attuned to reality than certain Marxist orthodoxies of the time, also encouraged a flight forward into a conception of revolutionary strategy as a violent test of strength with the state. The failure of this attempt 'to transform the poor into proletarians and proletarians into a liberation army' did not lead Negri down the path of resignation. What seems to have happened instead is that he eventually came to a residual conception of politics as a strategic field. In the age of Empire, revolutionaries no longer need to distinguish tactics and strategy, position and manoeuvre, weak links and invulnerable ones; they can now rely on a pervasive, if diffuse, popular desire for liberation and an episodic intuition of friend and enemy.

Alex Callinicos provides a critical reconstruction of Negri's career as a leading figure and theoretician of the Italian Autonomia movement. Callinicos diagnoses what he sees as the strategic myopia of this most militant wing of the Italian Far Left, as it flew headlong into futile and ultimately fatal clashes with the state, the Communist Party and the unions. Negri's rejection of the organized working class in favour of those on the margins of the labour market as the new subject of revolutionary politics found its expression in a conception of capitalism devoid of objective developmental tendencies. Callinicos maintains that it is imperative for Italy's renascent and boisterous radical scene to take a harder look at this legacy. *Empire*, in his view, has an obvious appeal in a milieu where paralyzing cynicism has been banished, but often at the expense of the ability to make a dispassionate assessment of the balance of forces at large, let alone conceive of a path to power.

While older class and national liberation struggles sent long-lasting shock waves across the interstate system, in the optic of *Empire* contemporary intifadas are of brief duration, media dependent, and do not fan out across national, let alone global, worlds of labour. In this celebrated age of communication, struggles have become all but incommunicable. Such a penetrating and sombre image of serialized outbursts of class anger warrants in-depth treatment. Undaunted by the sheer difficulty of even imagining the conditions under which large-scale class solidarities could re-emerge, the authors simply discount it as a problem. They suggest that such concerns are irrelevant to rebellions against the Empire that even now effectively capitalize on the symbolic logic of postmodern politics. In this alternative space, world history unfolds as a sequence of nearly magical serendipities. For happily, although local struggles no longer trigger off horizontal, upwardly spiralling revolutionary sequences, they can now immediately catapult up to the global level as unforeseen media events. By this more direct vertical route, the virtual centre of Empire can be attacked at any point.

For just because Empire is a media-steered system of political publicity, it is permanently vulnerable to the impact of destabilizing, marginal events that slip out of the control of those who manufacture consent. Empire is a society of the spectacle, seemingly powered by the pursuit of happiness – but in reality based on the mobilization of desires that are intimately wedded to the fear of failure, exclusion and loneliness. This is the politics of the society of the spectacle, in which the masses seek only the most immediate experiences of empowerment and agency, even if these are only ever episodic.

This desire for individual power and security, in the judgement of Michael Rustin, is the antithesis of that structure of feeling which sustains the solidarities of the multitude, and it is difficult to see by what dialectic the former capsizes into the latter. The future of Empire, he suggests, is much darker than Hardt and Negri acknowledge – more Hobbesian than Spinozist. Intriguingly, Hardt and Negri suggest that this spectral social order, sustained by false promises, is void for the future – an abstractly framed moment when a great refusal suddenly becomes possible. The rhetoric of the text attempts to slot itself into the narrative of a possible event. In an excursus on Machiavelli, they maintain that the time has come to compose great manifestoes that pry open an empty space for transformative intervention and beckon the multitude to surge through. Taking their cue from Althusser, they reason that Machiavelli invoked the masses in the transcendent form of an ideal prince, because he assumed that collective action could only be imagined in the mediated form of a singular agent; but the task now is to demystify these ossified mediations – leaders, parties and unions – and reclaim their absconded power for the multitude. Stanley Aronowitz is sceptical that this defiant abstentionism could be empowering. Mobile networks of counter-Empire militants have found powerful allies in organized labor, and will find vastly more in the rank and file of a reactivated union movement. Developing this line of criticism, Tom Mertes questions Michael Hardt's verdicts on the World Social Forum held in the spring of 2002 in the Brazilian city of Porto Alegre. The drastic erosion of public power is no cause for celebration amongst those struggling to mobilize the dispossessed of the neo-liberal era. Even as they reach out beyond the terrain of the nation-state in an arduous effort at constructing global solidarities, the variance in the collective experience of activists, operating in the qualitatively distinct zones of world capitalism, presents the decisive problem for an effective anti-capitalist politics. This problem is thoroughly effaced in Hardt's vision of effortless resistance in a stateless global order.

But to tax the authors with vexing questions of strategy might perhaps be unfair – a category mistake with regard to genre. Timothy Brennan's suggestion that Hardt and Negri have constructed a Sorelian myth underscores the prophetic aspirations of Empire. Indeed a line from Spinoza encapsulates the goal of the book: the prophet creates his own people. But Machiavelli's thoughts on prophecy strike a different note – one largely absent in this text – far from the comforts of any liberation theology, old or new.

> It must be considered that there is nothing more difficult to carry out, nor more doubtful of success, nor more dangerous to handle, than to initiate a new order of things. For the reformer has an enemy in all those who profit by the old order, and only lukewarm defenders in all those who would profit from the new order, this lukewarmness arising partly from fear of their adversaries, who have the laws in their favour; and partly from the incredulity of mankind, who do not believe in anything new until they have had actual experience of it.

We scarcely need to be reminded of the conclusion: all armed prophets have conquered, and unarmed ones failed.

In the 1970s, Negri might have understood this passage as a

clarion call for frontal collisions with the state. Decades later, *Empire* offers by contrast an optimism of the will that can only be sustained by a millenarian erasure of the distinction between the armed and the unarmed, the powerful and the abjectly powerless. From an ironically indeterminate political standpoint, free of any conventional progressive allegiances, Malcolm Bull challenges *Empire*'s account of the constituent power of the multitude for its inability to take cognizance of the reality of powerlessness. To their Spinozist notion of a boundless capacity to form and reform the order of human things, Bull counterposes a disconcerting ethic of unobtrusive mutuality, beyond phantasies of victorious empowerment.

What in the real world could Hardt and Negri point to as confirmation of the primal power of the seemingly helpless multitude? The answer comes into view only near the end of the work: Empire, seemingly in control everywhere, is unable to bridle the planetary flow of workers seeking jobs and a better life in rich countries. Reshaping social relations everywhere, immigration on this scale reveals, in their view, both the hostility of the multitude to the system of national borders and its tenacious desire for cosmopolitan freedom. This image of insurgent power as exodus conjoins the history of resistance that overturned New World slavery with the more recent experience of the collapse of the Soviet bloc. Although stirring as an emblem of agency, upon closer examination it dissolves into the grittier survival ethic that drives contemporary immigration.

In keeping with its ontological background, *Empire* does not develop any sustained programme for the injured and insulted of the world. Logically, however, its most distinctive proposal (the right to a guaranteed basic income occupies second place) is for abolition of all immigration controls: *papiers pour tous!* For Hardt and Negri, this is a demand that opens up the possibility of rejuvenating the politically stagnant core of global capitalism. But the desire to live, work and raise families in more affluent lands arguably finds its true manifesto in the inscription at the foot of the Statue of Liberty, holding out the promise of entirely prosaic freedoms.

But while Hardt and Negri downplay the mailed fist of the US in the global arena, they grant America a more gratifying central-ity as a laboratory of domestic political innovation. As they see it, both the thesis and the antithesis of Empire lie in the inclusive, expansive republicanism of the US Constitution, which long ago shed the European fetish of a homogeneous nation. Their conception of the Constitution as the original script of democratic self-determination is perhaps far-fetched: no modern charter can rival it for protecting wealth and privilege from the caprice of electorates. Yet it is arguably not the juristic form that is being described, but rather another myth. Hegel anticipated its basic structure of feeling – 'America is the country of the future, and its world historical importance has yet to be revealed in the ages which lie ahead . . . It is the land of desire for all those who are weary of the historical arsenal of old Europe'. In an era that extends from Tocqueville to Gramsci, American ascendancy could be plausibly linked to the retreat of old Europe before a menacing – alternately liberating – revolt of the masses. Indeed its Bolshevik enemy 'heard the siren song of Americanism most clearly. The challenge was to replicate the results of the capitalism that had achieved its pinnacle in the United States'. During the second half of the last century, America lost its primacy as the land of the most advanced forces of production, and descended to the level of its competitors in the OECD zone: what now explains its still resilient status as the hegemonic exemplar of western capitalism? A military hyperpower, a model of both unalloyed capitalism and multicultural accommodation, a mass culture with nearly universal appeal – these are the elements of an organic formula of hegemony that will be tested in the coming years. *Empire* is a bold attempt to capture the latest phase of its development, and an opportunity to revisit older traditions, and rediscover their actuality. A question from Gramsci pinpoints the stakes of the contention surrounding the work:

> The question [is] whether Americanism can constitute an historical 'epoch', that is whether it can determine a gradual evolution of the 'passive revolution' . . . typical of the last century, or whether on the other hand it does not simply represent the molecular accumulation of elements destined to produce an 'explosion' on the French pattern.

Empire:
A Postmodern Theory of Revolution

Michael Rustin

At a time when globalization has become an increasing focus for political movements of different kinds – effervescent demonstrations in the cities where congresses take place, and sustained campaigns for international agreements on debt or climate change – it is significant that a major treatise has appeared which attempts to give a coherent theoretical shape to global conflicts. *Empire* by Michael Hardt and Antonio Negri is a rare thing in the present age, a systematic treatise in political theory which sets out an argument for revolution.[1] Much of its interest lies in its systematicity – whether or not one agrees with its philosophical presuppositions, or with its socio-historical analysis, it is invaluable to see such an argument being constructed from first principles. Just as liberal philosophers like Rawls or Nozick have set out systematic political philosophies from their foundational principles of individual rights and freedoms, so Hardt and Negri have sought to find systematic grounds for their utopian conception of revolution. For this they have looked to construct an ambitious post-Marxist synthesis of ideas whose most important single source is the work of Deleuze and Guattari, but which draws also on 'republican' political theory, Foucault, Spinoza and Marx, among other sources. *Empire* establishes a systematic and grounded argument for a transformative view of the present historical situation, from a revolutionary perspective, and one does not have to agree with its arguments to recognize it as a landmark in contemporary political theory.

What is 'Empire'? This complex idea is Hardt and Negri's summation of the present state of world historical development, in terms of its system of governance, its mode of production, its forms of socialization and subjective identity, and its potentials for transformation. Hardt and Negri share with – indeed take from – Hegel and Marx a teleological theory of historical development, in which each new stage of evolution creates the potential for a fuller expression of human potential. They also share with Marx the idea that transitions from one stage of development to another are likely to be explosive, occasioned by crises and sudden transformations in popular consciousness. Marx explained this process largely by reference to the development of the means of production, and the overcoming of scarcity that this made possible. The advance of capitalist forms of production across the globe was a transitional stage for Marx in the later emergence of socialist forms of life. Hardt and Negri's analysis also gives priority to the global diffusion of capitalism, but they are less interested in its material than in its political, juridical, cultural and subjective dimensions. Where for Marx the alienation and eventual reclamation of human productive powers were the principal issue, for Hardt and Negri the political and subjective dimensions of the appropriation of human powers is at least as important.

Hardt and Negri's thinking has been shaped by Foucault and by Deleuze and Guattari as well as by Marxist political economy, and they give as much attention to changing forms of governmentality as to changing forms of production. 'The space of imperial sovereignty', they argue, 'is smooth'. What they mean by this is that the various boundaries and barriers, not least those of national sovereignties, are being swept away by global capitalism. This creation of 'one world', with no 'outside', as they put it, creates a potentially unified space in which the liberation of 'the multitude' by its own action becomes possible. Hardt and Negri seem more anarchist than Marxist in their identification of governmental powers, not economic exploitation, as the main obstacles to human liberation. 'Empire' also signifies an emergent form of global governance, but we will consider this later.

They bring together in their analysis of Empire a number of different discourses.[2] From neo-Marxist political economy is brought an analysis of the post-Fordist, post-industrial revolution.

The loss of hegemony of industrial production, and its partial supercession by an economy based on information and affect, is, in the authors' view, transforming the labour process and creating a much greater potential for mass resistance, and for the reappropriation of their own labour power by citizens, than was possible within the previous industrial regime. The argument here is that the 'virtual' character of much modern production, and the importance of symbolic production, especially the media, invests power in active subjects and thereby removes it from the owners and controllers of material resources. This transformation of the labour process, and the new emphasis within it on knowledge and affect (the latter arising from the increased weight of activities focused on health, education, social care in the post modern economy), together with the lessening constraints of time and space central to globalization, are creating, in Hardt and Negri's view, 'a new proletariat', 'the entire co-operating multitude'.[3]

A second strand of Hardt and Negri's argument derives from their theory of the state. Although the authors insist that they are libertarian communists, and not anarchists,[4] their view of the state is recognizably an anarchist one. Most forms of state power, in their view, alienate the autonomy of subjects and crush their creative power. They develop a historical argument which identifies radical and conservative poles in Enlightenment thinking and explains how the radical end of this antithesis – 'revolutionary humanism' – was defeated, with dire consequences for collective self-determination. 'The revolution of European modernity ran into its Thermidor'.[5] Enlightenment thus initiated not popular self-rule, but forms of sovereignty external to and 'other' than the subjects in whose name sovereign states claimed to govern. Doctrines of transcendence merely transferred authority from one displaced abstraction – God – to another – Man. The mind–body split instituted by Descartes defeated, in terms of influence, the immanentist doctrine of Spinoza, and this led to another damaging kind of alienation. The British empiricist tradition, with Hobbes at its centre, was particularly lethal in its consequences for the idea of creative self-rule, since it posited the necessity for the delegation of human powers for the preservation of peace and security. Subsequent mitigations of the extremity of this position, in Lockean theories of constitutional government constrained by the natural rights of citizens, and later in the theory

and practice of representative democracy, did not in Hardt and
Negri's view repair the fundamental flaws of this view of sovereignty, whose essence is that subjects are ruled and do not rule
themselves.

Empire brings together with this philosophical critique of sovereignty a Foucauldian argument concerning the changes in the
forms of power and control which have been exercised over
society. Foucault is one of the most important influences on
Hardt and Negri's work – they cast much of their historical
analysis in terms of a 'genealogy' of present formations. They take
from Foucault in particular the idea of 'a historical, epochal
passage in social forms from *disciplinary society* to the *society of
control*.[6] Disciplinary society is constructed through 'apparatuses
that produce and regulate customs, habits and productive practices'. This work of control is accomplished through disciplinary
institutions such as 'the prison, the factory, the asylum, the
hospital, the university, the school and so forth'. They argue that
this paradigm of power ruled throughout the first phase of
capitalist accumulation. By contrast, the society of control is one
'which develops at the far edge of modernity and opens towards
the postmodern' and is one in which 'mechanisms of command
become ever more "democratic", ever more immanent to the
social field'. Social control becomes interiorized within subjects
themselves. It is exercised directly on the minds and bodies of
subjects, through information systems and welfare practices.[7] It
thus extends well outside 'the structured sites of social institutions' into the fabric of everyday life. This amounts to a form
of 'bio-power' that regulates life from the interior of subjects,
a power which they 'embrace and reactivate' from their own
accord.[8]

There is a parallel – indeed a fusion – between the 'virtual'
and 'immanent' properties of labour in the post-industrial economy, and the 'interiorized' forms of control of the new kind of
governmentality. Hardt and Negri are describing a destruction or
compression of many previous differences and boundaries. Their
description of this process is hardly precise – 'the increasingly
intense relationship of mutual implication of all social forces that
capitalism has pursued throughout its development has now been
fully realised'. But whereas earlier Marxist writers such as those of
the Frankfurt School equated this 'real subsumption of labour

under capital' as a one-dimensional and potentially totalitarian process, Hardt and Negri, drawing on Foucault, take a contrary and more positive view of it. 'Civil society is absorbed in the state, but the consequence of this is an explosion of the elements that were previously coordinated and mediated in civil society.' Calling on Deleuze and Guattari, they argue that 'resistances are no longer marginal but active in the centre of a society that opens up in networks; the individual points are singularised in a thousand plateaus'.[9] The idea that the subjectivization of power, and the virtualization of production, creates the opportunity for new kinds of immanent resistance, connecting unpredictably and with immense potential through the 'rhizomes' of network society, is the essential basis of Hardt and Negri's revolutionary optimism. If one puts their account in the framework of complexity theory,[10] they model a complex but inherently increasingly unstable system, which has the potential to tip suddenly from one alienated kind of equilibrium of control to a different potential for liberation.

Their synthesis of a theory of changing forms of governmentality and sovereignty, with their analysis of post-industrial capitalism, allows them to see Empire as both a new system of power-relations, and a highly vulnerable one. In the latter more apocalyptic sections of the book, Empire is described as a parasitic formation, whose supercession as a global regime only awaits the awakening of the multitude to recognition of their immanent powers. But, in earlier chapters, the idea of Empire is elaborated in more positive terms, as an immanent emergent concept of global governance.[11] *Empire* was written, as its authors explain, after the Gulf War and before the Kosovo War. Its authors convinced themselves in that context that wars could now be waged only on behalf of some version of universal right and that in this sense some kind of global polity had already become fact.[12] They distinguish their concept of 'Empire' as a universal polity, from the European colonial empires, and from those respects in which the current world, dominated by the US, still resembles a conventional empire.[13] The difference between 'Empire' in their new sense, and the European empires, is that the European empires defined themselves in relation to the 'other' and inferior peoples whom they subjugated, and were also of course in competition with one another. The emerging 'global' Empire has no 'other'.[14] Just as capitalism as Marx predicted is now incorporating the entire globe into its systems, so the global polity is becoming similarly inclusive. In their own way, Hardt and Negri share the view of defenders of global capitalism such as Francis Fukuyama that 'the end of history' has now arrived, since in their view there is now nothing significant that lies outside the existing regimes of production and governance.

Just as with the internal order of states Hardt and Negri distinguish between alienating forms of sovereignty, and a revolutionary humanist order which presupposes government as a process of self-realization, so they distinguish between two traditions of international governance. One – the order of sovereign nation-states promulgated in the Treaty of Westphalia of 1648 – confines sovereignty within structured territorial domains. The other, the idea of 'perpetual peace' defined by Kant, imagines a universal order governed by common norms and entitlements, which morally override the claims of sovereign governments. They argue that this latter conception is beginning to become a reality as a consequence of a unified global economic order, and of the weakening and mutual interdependence of individual nation-states in the face of problems which confront them all. Their position recalls the arguments of writers such as David Held,[15] who have drawn attention to the vast increase in intergovernmental organizations and treaties in recent years, and to the increased sway of international law, as evidence that a new era of global governance is dawning. Hardt and Negri attach considerable importance to the United Nations, flawed though it is, to the role of non-governmental organizations (NGOs), and to the theory and practice of international jurists, in making the case.

They provide an unconvincingly rosy description of the uniqueness of the constitutional basis of the United States to justify the view that the hegemony of the US today is different from that of earlier empires. Its constitution is, they claim, expansive and inclusive, rather than restrictive and exclusive. Its idea of a balance of constitutional powers, which they compare with the model of constitutional balance which Polybius saw embodied in ancient Rome, leads them to advance the US Republic as a form of post-sovereign government, in which 'the multitude' expresses its powers through different contesting and complementary agencies (the federal principle and the famous separation of powers) and does not surrender or delegate them to some separate and other entity. This seems, as a description of current corrupted and plutocratic US constitutional practice, quite preposterous.

Although there are some parallels between Hardt and Negri's account of the emerging global order, and those of liberal internationalists such as Giddens and Held, they differentiate their own position from that more meliorist one. Whereas the liberal tradition looks forward to a regulated system of sovereignties, all subject to the sway of some universal juridical and ethical principles, Hardt and Negri hold the door open to a more total system-transformation, between what one might call actually-existing Empire and post-Empire. The global diffusion of information, and the repossession of powers by subjects within the new systems of non-material production and internalized regulation, create the possibility for new kinds of resistance and indeed uprising. They draw a striking analogue between the transformation of the universal aspiration of the ancient Roman Empire to constitute all of the civilized world into the universalist and inclusive claims of Christianity for equality before God (of all believers, one should add) and what might now be possible in terms of mobilization within the emergent order of global Empire. To put this in an older terminology, the multitude, which is being constituted by the global capitalist world order as a class in itself, can now seize the moment to assert itself as a class for itself. Hardt and Negri's view that the erosion of traditional forms of mediation and boundary (those of state sovereignty, for example) constitute opportunities for new forms of collective rcognition and mobilization make them emphatically repudiate any form of radical politics that looks backwards historically, even to past moments of relative success. They reject any politics based on nostalgia for earlier compromises, for example those achieved within national welfare states. They share with the post-socialists of the 'Third Way' the view that we now have to accept a new individualized, globalized, networked society as the only possible basis for future action, though the action they envisage is apocalyptic where the reformist post-socialists seek only to mitigate and regulate somewhat the turbulences of global capitalism, to which they envisage no conceivable alternative.[16]

The politics of *Empire*

How should we assess this ambitious account of our situation, and what conclusions can we draw from it in regard to questions of agency? Hardt and Negri's description of the major trends of development of both the capitalist economy, and of its major forms of governance, is plainly in accord with much current analysis of globalization. Shifts between economic sectors, the dominant role of the information economy, the 'subjectivization' of life, not least through the salience of consumption, and the weakening of insulating and defensive boundaries of many kinds, including those provided by the nation-state at its zenith, are well attested, and are now almost an orthodoxy in social theory. The contentious issue is not whether a transformation and hegemonization of consumer capitalism has been taking place, but whether this justifies the political argument that Hardt and Negri draw from it, to the effect that the economic system has now generated a universal proletariat.

A similar question can be asked about the erosion of sovereignty, and the exposure of populations to the effects of more geographically distant forms of power, through markets of many kinds, the global flows of information, people, commodities, etc. Is this to be understood, as Hardt and Negri suggest, as a potentially liberating process, since it constitutes a potentially unified multitude, in place of discrete, non-communicating and often mutually hostile segments? Does the fact that more than ever before populations inhabit 'the same world' – that is to say, the same complex open system – signify that they do or can acquire a common consciousness as universal citizens or labourers? Do Hardt and Negri successfully refute the alternative, more pessimistic view, which is that these homogenizing factors have created not a creative and cooperative multitude, but an atomized 'mass society', vulnerable more than ever before to manipulation from above?

Although Hardt and Negri do pose the problematic of the transformation of Empire in somewhat traditional terms, in their evocations of a universal proletariat and 'common multitude', there is a contradiction between their post-Marxist, but still in some ways traditional, formulation of directional change, and the forms of social action to which their analysis actually points.

Although they posit a potential unity of the subjugated, the examples of radical action which they cite are anything but unitary. Melville's Bartleby, Coetzee's Michael X, the International Workers of the World (IWW), myriad refugees and migrant labourers, St Francis of Assisi and St Augustine are figures who have little in common, except being instances of 'constituent' (or prefigurative) activity, in some instances the activity only of passive resistance or bare survival. Hardt and Negri are hostile to all constituted limits to human action – to the principle of authority itself – and it follows that any political movement which began to constitute itself as a positive programme, with its own embryonic institutions, would become deeply self-contradictory in their eyes.

There is a kind of social action which does follow from this description of society. It is self-active, self-constituting, often negative, highly competitive, driven by the desire for free expression and power. The 22-year-old graduate who sets up his own computer business in Silicon Valley may be as much an exemplar of this spirit as the NGO worker trying to prevent a famine, though their ethics are different. Some change in the postmodern world is indeed transmitted by these 'rhizomatic' means, by networks, and the virus-like replication and mutation of kinds of actions outside the control of formal structures and hierarchies. This is the sociological truth of Hardt and Negri's account. The political appeal of their analysis, its natural constituency so to speak, is to those called by 'desire' in its various forms, and moved by hostility to restriction and restraint, not to the would-be builders of new systems and structures. Global capitalism has been the bringer of this condition of freedom. It is this which has created, against the opposition of sovereignties, the 'smooth space' in which fluidity and mobility become a general condition of life. Hardt and Negri are antagonistic to capitalism, and how could the boundary-free space which they celebrate survive without it?

The question of human nature

One issue in coming to conclusions about the consequences of the loss of boundaries is the contribution which the innate features of human nature make to social arrangements. Hardt and Negri take a postmodern view of this question, arguing that human nature is a legacy of modern 'dualisms' which postulated 'outsides' to human freedom in order to justify imposing limits to it.[17] Although they may therefore regard the idea of human nature as outmoded, they make the assumption that, given freedom and creative possibility, human beings will construct a cooperative and expressive world. The fact that people have not always acted in this spirit is not to be explained by inherent ambivalence in the innate human imputs, but by defective, alienating and exploitative social arrangements. 'Man is born free, but everywhere is in chains' would be one way of putting their underlying assumption.[18]

Consider in this connection Hardt and Negri's challenging account of the Thermidorian defeat of revolutionary humanism in the early years of the Enlightenment. (This is one of the many fertile avenues for thought opened up by this book.) Hardt and Negri seek to rescue the revolutionary tradition of republican self-determination, closely linked with Machiavelli, from neglect, and from its customary subordination to positivistic theories of law and sovereignty.[19] They do not, however, ask why this defeat took place, and why the arguments of the Hobbesian tradition (or of defences of the state in other traditions, such as that of Hegel) have in fact proved so historically effective.

Marx did offer one persuasive explanation of why these successive defeats of universal aspirations, embodied in the experience of successive emergent social classes, had taken place. His explanation focused on the effects of scarcity, in making unavoidable the appropriation of the means of production by the collective self-interst of classes, rather than by humanity as a whole. Thus, once scarcity had been overcome by the full development of the means of production, there was reason to believe that the historical usurpation of the general interest by sectional classes could be transcended. Although this argument does not explain as much as Marxists supposed, and although its use as a justification for political action has often been both reductionist and oppressive, it nevertheless retains considerable explanatory force. It is, for example, impossible to imagine any inclusive democratic world system being established whilst the differences in economic well-being between peoples remain as they are.

Hardt and Negri do not, however, deploy this long-established Marxian theorem. (Perhaps they take it as a given.) Instead, they are more interested in what happens in the domain of desire, will, understanding and affect, and in what can be expected from transformations at this level. This element of their argument comes from a quite different tradition, via the work of Foucault and Deleuze and Guattari. Its earlier origins lie in writers such as Nietzsche and Bergson. What one might call its 'energetics' – the idea of a potential transformative force of will of the multitude – comes from this source, though it is transformed in Hardt and Negri's communist hands into a benign form which assumes that, external obstacles removed, human beings could then flower, in all their potential differences, in cooperative harmony with one another.

Suppose, however, that this underlying view of human nature is flawed and partial? And not only partial but also internally contradictory, since the marriage that Hardt and Negri attempt to effect between what one might think of as the 'right' and 'left' strands of their own theoretical formation (the Nietzschean and the Marxist) is given no explanation or justification. This is indeed a rather common contradiction in postmodern social theory, in which a radical leftist 'structure of feeling' has survived the demolition or abandonment of most of the beliefs (e.g. concerning human nature, determining structures, objective realities) on which transformative left politics originally depended, and perhaps must depend. We do indeed have to decide what we think human nature brings to the world before we can hope to understand what kind of world it can be.

Deleuze and Guattari conducted a brilliant and witty critique of Freud and Lacan in their *Anti-Oedipus*, whose central argument was that psychoanalysis had wrongly endorsed the inevitablity of repression in its account of human development and had condensed into its model of a necessary Oedpial renunciation in each generation the wider system of social authority – the 'law of the father', in Lacanian terms. They sought to rewrite psychoanalysis as one might say from the perspective of the id, invoking 'desiring machines' as potential subjects. Freud, however, thought there was an inherent problem in the regulation and reconciliation of human desires, both between and within generations. His actual position was not so different from that of Hardt and Negri's hero, Spinoza, in arguing that it was only understanding that could render such choices and renunciations tolerable both for individuals and for society.[20] Melanie Klein clarified these issues further in her investigations of early life and through her discovery of the dual drives or emotions of love and hate in the infant (she thought the balance of these was positively or negatively inflected by environment and nurture, but not solely an outcome of this) and the widespread prevalence of anxiety as a basic human propensity. This Kleinian postion, as I have tried to argue elsewhere, provides an essential foundation for political theory.[21] It is necessary, that is to say, to take account of both the negative and destructive potentials of human nature, as well as of its positive and creative potentials, in considering the systems of social organization that could bring about a better human existence.

The Hobbesian account of the state of nature, as a war of all against all, places its weight on the destructive side of this necessary dualism, and no 'progressive' social thinking can be based on that foundation. It is, however, as well to remember that Hobbes's account does address a part of reality – it describes what can happen if destructive forces are given full reign and no authority exists to contain them. It demonstrates that the minimum and necessary role of government is always to keep the peace and ensure security of life. One reason why the 'revolutionary humanist' tradition lost out to its Thermidorian rival is because this situation of fear and anxiety often obtained in reality, and sovereign authority had some effectiveness and won some consent in dealing with it.

The problem with Hardt and Negri's unrealistically optimistic view of human motivation is that such idealization is unavoidably accompanied by what Kleinian psychoanalysts called a splitting of good and bad, love and hate, the destructive and the creative. In Hardt and Negri's argument, this splitting involves the location of all destructive forces in external authorities and of all creative powers in subjugated individuals. Such demonization of authority, and idealization of its opponents, is a dangerous guide to political practice.

The political conjuncture of *Empire*

This brings us to the political moment of Hardt and Negri's book, which they explain to us 'was begun well after the end of the

Persian Gulf War, and completed well before the beginning of the war in Kosovo'.²² It was published in 2000 before the events of September 11, 2001. I think this timing must now influence one's reading of their argument.

The success the US may have had in the Gulf War crisis in presenting itself 'as the only power able to manage international justice *not as a function of its own national motives but in the name of global right*',²³ has not been repeated in the aftermath of September 11. Nor is it any longer obvious, as Hardt and Negri put it in discussing the Vietnam War, that 'the Tet offensive . . . marked the irreversible military defeat of the U.S. imperialist adventures'. The idea that the US, unique among preponderant powers, depends on international consent and universalist criteria to legitimate what it does, and is constrained by a new form of 'Empire', is at this point unconvincing. The present US government seems rather to have interpreted September 11 as an opportunity to demonstrate that its Vietnam defeat was an aberration – mainly the result of its own inhibitions and miscalculations – and that in future its military power can and will be deployed effectively wherever it is necessary, regardless of what other nation-states may wish. The 'peace' that the present US administration seeks to enforce refers to the suppression or deterrence of its own supposed enemies and seems to have no more general meaning than this. Its current unilaterialism is a direct repudiation of the universalist principles and practice that Hardt and Negri hailed as definitive of the governmental norms of 'Empire', in contrast to previous empires. At the very least, they have been premature in their welcoming of a new kind of world order.

One also needs to review the larger dynamics of September 11 and its aftermath in the light of Hardt and Negri's analysis. Unfortunately, when one considers the kinds of political action that might be expected to take place in the 'smooth' interconnected spaces of Empire, by globalized, subjectively empowered, rhizomatic networks, Al Qaeda seems to qualify for inclusion as much as NGO volunteers or journalists working in disaster areas.²⁴ Hardt and Negri say, evoking Nietzsche, that 'a new nomad horde, a new race of barbarians, will arise to invade or evacuate Empire'.²⁵ They refer to a 'new positive barbarism'. They quote Walter Benjamin: 'What does the poverty of experience oblige the barbarian to do? To begin anew, to begin from the new'.[26] They go on: 'What exists, he reduces to rubble, not for the sake of the rubble but for that of the way leading through it. The new barbarians destroy with affirmative violence, and trace new paths of life through their own material existence'.[27] It is unfortunately clear how references to 'rubble' may be read at this particular moment, long after they were written.

Hardt and Negri, however, make few useful distinctions between what kinds of interventions against Empire they are anticipating or inviting. In their concluding invocations of militancy,[28] they refer to the 'virtues of insurrectional action of two hundred years of experience', to the organizers of the IWW, to St Francis of Assisi and 'his joyous life including all of being and nature', and to the idea of turning 'rebellion into a project of love'. But there can be no serious political action which does not take differences of motivation seriously. The interventions of NGO volunteers, investigative journalists, or jurists, in a crisis such as Rwanda or Kosovo, evoke responses of indignation, compassion and solitarity, which are supportive of the recognition and enforcement of global ethical norms. More violent interventions tend to generate paranoid and vengeful reactions among both peoples and their governments. Such reactions are now authorizing possible military action by the US against no less than seven nations. The problem with the open, unstructured, globalized universe which Hardt and Negri celebrate is that it is liable to generate many different kinds of 'insurrectionary' action, which may include the various modes of carnival, witness, reparation and terror. Such actions may be visionary and prefigurative, or largely destructive. The unstable and volatile 'Empire' that Hardt and Negri describe may be capable of being transformed in different ways, either in the direction of the benign global governance they describe in their early chapters, or in the direction of extreme violence and retribution. These are alternative possibilities that Hardt and Negri do not explore, though they have now been brought into high focus by the events of September 11, or indeed those which have been taking place since then in Israel and the Palestinian territories.

The psychosocial consequences of capitalism

A third major problem in Hardt and Negri's argument is its underestimation of the problems which capitalism poses to the possibility of the inclusive and generous society they wish to see. Probably because of their postmodern rejection of materialist explanation, they underestimate the dominating power of capital, deterritorialized or not (it is much less deterritorialized than the authors suggest) and of its role as a covert ruling power. If the power of capital continues to constrain most forms of action across the globe, it matters little if it is now exercised in more abstract, spaceless and invisible ways. The 'destructuration' and loss of boundaries brought about by global capital brings dangers, as well as liberatory possibilities. New 'transversal' syntheses, hybrids and mobilities of all kinds are indeed a product of a more open and interpenetrated environment, and Hardt and Negri's postmodern celebration of this diversity has its point. But what may follow from the weakness of containing structures – whether provided by nation-states, firms, unions, governments, families or territorial communities – is not a new sense of freedom, but intensified levels of anxiety, expressed as hostility towards foreigners, enemies, migrants, differences of all kinds. This feeling of vulnerability and exposure to danger explains both the current conformist mood of US public opinion in relation to its perceived enemies, and the xenophobic shift to the right which is taking place among voters across Europe. The idea that such states of uncertainty and fear are likely to lead to new global solidarities, and to support for Hardt and Negri's 'transitional programme'[29] seems improbable.

Capitalism is an engine which generates anxiety and fear as its normal concomitants. Its continuous invasion of limits and boundaries (which Hardt and Negri hail as progressive, since it has already destroyed the European colonial empires and is now including the peoples of the entire globe in the 'new proletariat') exposes not only labourers and citizens but even capitalists themselves to continuous risk and danger. Individuals and groups may react to these threats in the universalist and solidaristic ways that Hardt and Negri hope for, but there are other possibilities and precedents. Further, aggression is an instinct necessary for survival in the capitalist market, and the more exposed the markets, the greater the pressures to be aggressive. The violence of which a state such as the US is capable, both towards its own deviants and its perceived external enemies, derives from its own dominant principle of existence. It has seemed surprising that the triumph of global capitalism over its communist rival in 1989 should have been followed by an intensifaction, rather than a diminution, of fear and anxiety. We have never been in greater danger than now, President Bush has recently said, which considering that the earlier danger was of massive nuclear attack is remarkable.[30] It may even be that the more unfettered and triumphant capitalism is, the higher the levels of underlying anxiety and fear to which it gives rise. This may also explain why it is that US administrations, which have been the most fundamentalist in their commitments to capitalism, and the least influenced by countervailing values, have also been the most paranoid in their views of the world.

Hardt and Negri draw attention to an emergent state of de-structuration, as the *Communist Manifesto*'s aphorism – 'all that is solid melts into air' – is nearer to becoming reality. They may, however, misjudge its most likely outcomes. Unstable, exposed and turbulent conditions more often lead to catastrophic than utopian outcomes. The events of September 11 may yet prove to have been the triggering of just such a destabilization. An awak-ening and insurgency of the multitude is one possible conse-quence of such a situation, but it does not seem the most likely one. Alternatively, the outcome of September 11 could yet prove to be a Third World War, arising perhaps from the kinds of serial blundering that led to the Great War in 1914. There is little sign that these authors, admittedly at a more peaceful time of writing, had these darker possibilities of Empire in their minds.

Notes

1. Michael Hardt and Antonio Negri, *Empire*, Cambridge, MA: Harvard University Press, 2000. In this essay, Empire or 'Empire' with a capital E will refer to Hardt and Negri's use of the term, *Empire* to the book itself.

2. Some of these have been set out in the writers' earlier works, e.g. Antonio Negri, *The Politics of Subversion: A Manifesto for the Twenty-First Century*, trans. James Newall, Cambridge: Polity 1989; Antonio Negri, *The Savage Anomaly*, trans. Michael Hardt, Minneapolis: University of Minnesota Press 1991; Michael Hardt and Antonio Negri, *Labor of Dionysus*, Minneapolis:

Minnesota University Press, 1994; and Paolo Virno and Michael Hardt (eds), *Radical Thought in Italy*, Minneapolis: University of Minnesota Press 1996.
3. *Empire*, p. 402. A curious feature of their argument is that, whereas Marx thought the road to class solidarity and revolution lay in the socialization of the production process, Hardt and Negri derive this possibility from what is in many respects an individualization of the labour process.
4. Ibid., p. 350.
5. Ibid., p. 75.
6. Ibid., p. 23.
7. So far as those who work in these systems are concerned, the evidence is that these 'interiorised forms of control' are effective rather than otherwise. The training and compliance procedures now ubiquitous in their management – competency-based learning, quality assurance and the like – impose tight control of these labour processes, and are inimical to free thinking.
8. *Empire*, pp. 23–4.
9. *Empire*, p. 25. This is a reference to Gilles Deleuze and Félix Guattari, *A Thousand Plateaus*, London: Athlone 1988.
10. See David Bryne, *Complexity Theory and the Social Sciences*, London: Routledge 1998.
11. The difference in tone and assumption between these sections is very striking and suggests that it may derive from differences of approach between the two authors.
12. As they put it, 'the importance of the Gulf War derives rather from the fact that it presented the USA as the only power able to manage international justice *not as a function of its own national motives but in the name of global right*' (p. 180, emphasis in original).
13. There are, of course, important differences between the forms of territorial domination effected by the US, and by the European colonial empires. But at this point these seem to have more to do with strategic interests and forms of mediating power (capital, long-distance weaponry, the purchase of governments, in contrast to trade and direct territorial occupation) than with the contrast Hardt and Negri seek to make between old imperial power and some new deterritorialized form of global order.
14. In fact, it is has been constructing Islam as an other for itself, indicating that 'otherness' continues to have its uses.
15. See David Held, Anthony McGrew, David Goldblatt and Jonathan Perraton, *Global Transformations: Politics, Economics and Culture*, Cambridge: Polity 1999.
16. Hardt and Negri are not only hostile to defensive nationalisms, but also show no interest in the construction of new governmental frames like that of the European Union through which peoples might be defended from market risks and uncertainties. Within their framing of the issue, the most 'modern' society, whose members come nearst to constituting the new 'multitude', seems on the contrary to be that of the US.
17. They quote (p. 187) Fredric Jameson: ' "Postmodernism" is what you have when the modernisation process is complete and nature is gone for good'.
18. They are, however, critical of Rousseau, regarding his concept of the 'general will' as a conservative, proto-nationalist idea.

19. They follow Gramsci in finding in Machiavelli the key source for a modern theory of consensual self-government.
20. This is not, however, how Hardt and Negri read Spinoza's philosophy.
21. See Michael Rustin, *The Good Society and the Inner World*, London: Verso 1991; and Michael Rustin, *Reason and Unreason*, London: Continuum 2001.
22. *Empire*, p. xvii.
23. Ibid., p. 180.
24. Manuel Castells, in the second volume of his *Information Age* trilogy, *The Power of Identity*, Oxford: Blackwell 2000, was prescient in recognizing that social movements came in many varieties, progressive and reactionary.
25. *Empire*, p. 213.
26. Ibid., p. 216.
27. Ibid., p. 215.
28. Ibid., pp. 411–13.
29. Its components are 'the right to global citizenship', 'the right to a social wage' and 'the right to reappropriation' (of the means of production). The right to education and information might usefully be added to this list.
30. It is noteworthy that a concept of security based on mutual deterrence served to manage anxieties about the Soviet Union, within that rather highly structured contest, but is deemed irrelevant to the containment of so relatively weak a state as Iraq.

The New World Order

Stanley Aronowitz

The United States never held a large number of direct colonies, a fact that has prompted many political leaders to declare it the great exception to colonialism. Yet the Monroe Doctrine was for a century and a half a rallying cry for American economic and military engagement in Central and South America, and, fuelled by Cold War considerations, it remained a hallmark of American foreign policy into the nineties. And for many, the Vietnam War was emblematic of US imperialism: consistent with its Cold War foreign policy, the United States assumed the role of protector of a weak, antidemocratic but anti-communist regime and intervened to thwart the self-determination of the Vietnamese people, especially when they chose to live under communist rule. Even the collapse of Eastern European communism and the rapidly proceeding integration of China into the world market have failed to stem the steady tide of US military intervention into the affairs of smaller, quasi-sovereign nations.

While the rhetoric of anti-communism has given way to the rhetoric of human rights as a justification for involvements such as the Gulf War and the Kosovo War, for many these are merely continuing examples of the same old imperialist adventures. But according to Antonio Negri and his American collaborator Michael Hardt, the Vietnam War was the last great battle of the old imperialism. In their view we have entered the era of Empire, a 'supranational' centre consisting of networks of transnational corporations and advanced capitalist nations led by the one remaining superpower, the United States. In this new, globalized economic and political system, a genuine world market has been created, national boundaries are increasingly porous and a new system of 'imperial authority' is in the process of taking hold.

The new paradigm of Empire 'is both system and hierarchy, centralized construction of norms and far-reaching production of legitimacy, spread out over world space'. The invocation of human rights is not merely a fig leaf for the imperium; it is part of an effort to create enforceable international law in which the institutions of Empire take precedence over formerly sovereign states – in short, assume the role of world court as well as policeman.

While by no means minimizing the fact that the United States stands at the pinnacle of the new system, Hardt and Negri insist that the project is one of creating a system in which disputes between nations are adjudicated by a legitimate international authority and by consensus, upon which world policing may be premised. Even though the institutions are not in place – most of the initiatives remain ad hoc, as is evident in Africa at this very moment – the authors announce the existence of a dominant 'systemic totality' or logic that, however invisible, regulates the new economic and political order that has taken hold almost everywhere. The new paradigm of Empire has gained enormous strength since the collapse of the Soviet Union, but it is not the direct result of Cold War triumph. It emerged organically within the old system as a result of the tremendous power of the postwar labour movements to bid up both wages and the social wage, the pressure of national liberation movements on the old imperialism and the gradual delegitmation of nation-states and their institutions to maintain internal cultural as well as political discipline.

Having increased its power at the old industrial workplace, by the sixties labour was engaged in what Negri has previously termed 'the refusal to work'. Even as mass consumption was rising, productivity eroded, and profits in some instances actually declined. The nation-state – which since the great eighteenth- and nineteenth-century revolutions had, through education, citizenship for the lower social classes and imperial ideologies such as racism and patriotism, been effective in enforcing internalized mass discipline – was increasingly unable to command popular allegiance as, one after another, efforts to thwart Third World national liberation movements ran aground. Things came to a head in 1968 and 1969 when mass strikes, notably in France and Italy, almost toppled sitting governments; disruptions and mass demonstrations also threatened the stability of regimes in Mexico and the United States. The authors argue that the conjunction of economic crisis and the crisis of rule was an occasion for renewal, not breakdown. The renewal was signalled by President Nixon's early-seventies abrogation of the Bretton Woods agreement; the dollar rather than gold became the universal money standard. Weakened by international competition and rising costs of production and governance, it was no longer possible to contain world prices by monetary means and preserve the system of internal trade regulation. Now the dollar 'floated' along with other currencies. In quick succession, the United States removed most major regulatory controls: on banks, trucking and other transportation, and most antitrust restraints. Fuel prices and many others now floated in the market. While Nixon started the process of ending the stubborn legacy of the New Deal, the so-called Reagan revolution, which the Clinton administration extended, greatly accelerated the changes. The doctrine of Keynesianism, which proclaimed that since capitalism tended toward equilibrium below the level of full employment, governments must intervene directly to stimulate economic growth and employment, was declared dead. The free market, and with it the idea that government should as much as possible stay out of the economy, except to regulate the supply of money and credit in order to stem inflationary tendencies, became the new religion.

A key element in the new corporate strategy was to reduce wages by curbing the power of organized labour. Battered by the 'deterritorialization' of industrial production as corporations moved plants offshore and by relentless antilabour policies, by the eighties organized labor in all major industrial countries was in full retreat. In the United States and Britain, unions proved unable to prevent many features of the social wage (welfare-state benefits) won during the thirties and early postwar years. While the power of labour in other countries took a longer time to diminish, the nineties were years of agony for most European workers. Even when labour-backed socialist governments took power in France, Germany and Italy, welfare-state erosion, heavy losses in the old material-goods industries and the rise of largely non-union information and communications sectors reduced the power of organized labour and, with few exceptions, its will to resist governments' neo-liberal economic policies.

For Hardt and Negri, globalization was the major mechanism to solve the crisis. Three key transformations have occurred since the sixties: the shift in the economy from the dominance of industrial production to information; the integration of the world market so that, with global communications, industrial deterritorialization, accelerated world investment and trade, the lines are now blurred between 'inside and outside'; and the decline of the nation-state as the core of political sovereignty and as a mediator of economic and political protest. The introduction of new technologies led to the creation of entirely new communications and information industries, which have largely replaced the old regime of Fordist production. Fordism, which subjected the worker to rationalized tasks by transferring knowledge to machines – assembly lines and other methods – has largely been replaced with what has been termed 'Toyotaism', or post-Fordism. One of the characteristic features of the new production method is 'just in time' production. Through computerized information technologies, management is able to compress the time between the provision of raw materials to the shop floor and the actual production process.

But the technological revolution has had another effect. Information technology signifies the advent of 'immaterial' production, and with it the emergence of the worker who integrates knowledge, skill and labour – what Robert Reich has designated 'symbolic-analytic services', activities that entail 'problem-solving' and 'brokering', once performed chiefly by managers. The central actor in this new immaterial production no longer stands as a cog in the labour process but is at the centre of it. Since these workers are, contrary to popular belief, not immune to the vagaries of exploitation (many of them work on a part-time, contingent and temporary basis, even in software heartlands), they are among the potential actors in a potentially revived labour movement. Globalism is not primarily a regime of goods production but, with the aid of science, leads to a new paradigm of the relations of humans to the physical universe. Nature, too, has been integrated into the new system – witness the emergence of industries based on biotechnology that treat life as a new field for investment and production.

Nation-states, which emerged from the decline of the feudal monarchies and aristocracies and their replacement by liberal democratic systems, still perform important tasks for Empire. Without them the control of whole populations would be impossible. Yet imperialism has died precisely because nations are no longer the key mediators of international economics and politics. The nation may still ignite fierce loyalties among subordinate peoples, but for Hardt and Negri, it is no longer independent from the new world order.

Having destroyed the old colonial system by revolution and civil war, the legacy of newly decolonized states has been nothing short of tragic. Although the revolutionaries of Asia and Africa achieved national independence, they were never able to establish economic autonomy. During the Cold War some, like India, maintained a degree of independence by playing on the division between the two great powers; others allied themselves firmly on either side. China, under an often brutal revolutionary dictatorship, broke with both sides and tried to modernize by subjecting its own population to development by means of force. In almost none of these nations were the majority of their populations afforded decent living standards. In the year 2000 a third of the world's labour force remains unemployed or underemployed, and millions have migrated in order to make a living. The term 'Third World' describes the past. Having been subordinated to Empire, these nations no longer offer an alternative. Acknowledging the hardships suffered by victims of war, famine and unemployment, Hardt and Negri see a new proletariat emerging on a world scale out of the enormous exodus of peasants, a proletariat that may become one of the constituents of resistance against Empire. The old distinction between industrial production and agriculture has been sundered, as hundreds of millions of people are herded into cities. Those who remain on the land are increasingly subject to capitalist industrial methods, literally factories in the field.

Although *Empire* sometimes strays from its central theme, it is a bold move away from established doctrine. Hardt and Negri's insistence that there really is a new world is promulgated with energy and conviction. Especially striking is their renunciation of the tendency of many writers on globalization to focus exclusively on the top, leaving the impression that what happens down below, to ordinary people, follows automatically from what the great powers do. In the final chapters they try to craft a new theory of historical actors, but here they stumble, sometimes badly. The main problem is that they tend to overstate their case. From observations that the traditional forces of resistance have lost their punch, the authors conclude that there are no more institutional 'mediations'. Not so fast.

One of the serious omissions in *Empire*'s analysis is a discussion of the World Trade Organization, the International Monetary Fund and the World Bank, three of the concrete institutions of the repressive world government of Empire. Lacking an institutional perspective – except with respect to law – Hardt and Negri are unable to anticipate how the movement they would bring into being might actually mount effective resistance. Although not obliged to provide a programme for a movement, the authors do offer indicators of which social forces may politically take on the colossus. Having argued that institutions such as trade unions and political parties are no longer reliable forces of combat, they are left with the postmodern equivalent of the nineteenth-century proletariat, the 'insurgent multitude'. In the final chapters of the book, incisive prose gives way to hyperbole, and the sharp delineation of historical actors melts into a vague politics of hope. Insisting that 'resistance' precedes power, they advocate direct confrontation, 'with an adequate consciousness of the central repressive operations of Empire' as it seeks to achieve 'global citizenship'. At the end, the authors celebrate the 'nomadic revolutionary' as the most likely protagonist of the struggle.

The demonstrations against the WTO in Seattle in December 1999 and the subsequent anti-IMF and World Bank protests in Washington suggest a somewhat different story. The 40,000-plus demonstrators who disrupted the WTO meetings and virtually shut down the city consisted of definite social groups: a considerable fraction of the labour movement, including some of its top leaders, concerned that lower wages and human rights violations would both undermine their standards and intensify exploitation; students who have been protesting sweatshop labour for years and are forcing their universities to cease buying goods produced by it; and a still numerous, if battered, detachment of environmentalists – a burgeoning alliance that appears to have continued.

These developments shed light on the existence of resistance to Empire but also on the problem of theories that wax in high abstractions. Events argue that some of the traditional forces of opposition retain at least a measure of life. While direct confrontation is, in my view, one appropriate strategy of social struggle today, it does not relieve us of the obligation to continue to take the long march through institutions, to test their mettle. After all, 'adequate consciousness' does not appear spontaneously; it emerges when people discover the limits of the old. And the only way they can understand the nature of the new Empire is to experience the frustrations associated with attempts to achieve reforms within the nation-state, even as the impulse to forge an international labour/environmentalist alliance proceeds.

3

A Nebulous Empire

Charles Tilly

Empire's dust jacket features a satellite photo of spiralling white clouds above indistinct purple seas. Beyond the earth's edge, it displays black nothingness. The designer must have read the book. Although Saskia Sassen's endorsement describes it as: 'An extraordinary book, with enormous intellectual depth and a keen sense of the history-making transformation that is beginning to take shape', Michael Hardt and Antonio Negri orbit so far from the concrete realities of contemporary change that their readers see little but clouds, hazy seas and nothingness beyond. Behold their central claim: an invisibly virtual Empire (always capitalized and always singular) is now displacing and surpassing the capitalist state – even the United States of America – as the locus of world power. Territorial, racial, sexual and cultural boundaries cease to matter. 'With boundaries and differences suppressed or set aside,' Hardt and Negri declare, 'the Empire is a kind of smooth space across which subjectivities glide without substantial resistance or conflict'.[1] Moreover, the Empire's 'biopower' extends beyond tools, machines and organizations to bodies, thoughts and social life as a whole. Despite existing in no particular place, Empire exercises unitary agency. It advertises itself as history's eternal end.

That claim is false: in a new dialectic, *Empire* creates its antithesis in a connected multitude (never capitalized, but always singular) whose rising will eventually re-appropriate and transform imperial means of control. The organizing argument sounds global echoes of the *Communist Manifesto*. Unlike Marx and

Engels, however, Hardt and Negri consider their redeeming multitude to consist not of workers, not even of persons, but of 'productive, creative subjectivities of globalization'.[2] Much of the book's first half glosses nineteenth- and twentieth-century world history as a shift from European to American imperialism, with the United States as the new system's peace police but not its master. Resistance to American imperialism, in that gloss, destroyed American hegemony by connecting everyone with a worldwide network of capital. In the process, international migration became the principal means of class struggle; exploited people opted out. (Enthusiasm for this argument leads Hardt and Negri to dismiss nineteenth-century Atlantic migrations wrongly as 'Lilliputian' compared to their late twentieth-century counterparts; proportionately speaking, the 30 million Europeans and 9 million Africans who crossed the Atlantic exceeded today's international flows.) Their analysis aligns Hardt and Negri against other leftists who call for resistance to globalization, especially those who advocate local action against global forces. It also leads them to disparage defenders of nongovernmental organizations and new forms of international law – including the impeccably leftist Richard Falk – as dupes of institutions whose moral intervention actually advances the imperial work of globalization. As if that shucking off of potential sympathizers were insufficient, Hardt and Negri reject the stirring concreteness of the *Communist Manifesto*, making a virtue of that rejection. They cast their argument abstractly, in idiosyncratically defined terms, with few concrete illustrations of the social processes they have in mind. They insist, in fact, that the coming of Empire has annihilated all external criteria for judging political systems: 'In Empire, no subjectivity is outside, and all places have been subsumed in a general "non-place." The transcendental fiction of politics can no longer stand up and has no argumentative utility because we all exist entirely within the realm of the social and the political.'[3] As Hardt and Negri declare, such a position rules out conventional forms of measurement and evidence. A sceptical reader can nevertheless legitimately question the book's presumptions and assertions. Given the world's recent fragmentation, inequality and internecine conflict, what warrant have we for concluding that it is, as Hardt and Negri claim, rapidly becoming a seamless web of control? What process of capitalist conquest and infiltration could possibly have woven that web? How did capital activate its three alleged means of control – bombs, money, ether – and how did those three means produce their effects on the whole world's population? Is it true, for example, that expanded communication 'imposes a continuous and complete circulation of signs'?[4] Might we not have thought, on the contrary, that the Internet (currently accessible to about six per cent of the earth's population, with dramatic inequalities of information available to different segments of that six per cent) exacerbates discontinuities in the availability of information? Until we hear more about how Empire's causes produce their effects, it would be wise to retain a measure of scepticism.

Notes

1. Michael Hardt and Antonio Negri, *Empire*, Cambridge, MA: Harvard University Press 2000, p. 198.
2. Ibid., p. 60.
3. Ibid., p. 353.
4. Ibid., p. 347.

Lineages of Empire

Giovanni Arrighi

I

Michael Hardt and Antonio Negri's *Empire* is a powerful antidote
to the gloom, suspicion and hostility that have characterized the
predominant reaction of the radical left to the advent of so-called
globalization. While excoriating its destructive aspects, Hardt and
Negri welcome globalization as the dawn of a new era full of
promise for the realization of the desires of the wretched of the
earth. In the same way that Marx insisted on the progressive
nature of capitalism in comparison with the forms of society it
displaced, they now claim that Empire is a great improvement
over the world of nation-states and competing imperialisms that
preceded it.

Empire is the new logic and structure of rule that has emerged
with the globalization of economic and cultural exchanges. It is
the sovereign power that effectively regulates these global
exchanges and thereby governs the world. Unlike empires of premodern and modern times, the singular Empire of postmodern
times has no territorial boundaries or centre of power. It is a
decentred and *deterritorialized* apparatus of rule that incorporates
the entire global realm.

The establishment of this new logic and structure of rule has
gone hand in hand with 'the realization of the world market and
the real subsumption of global society under capital'.[1] The world
of nation-states and competing imperialisms of modern times

'served the needs and furthered the interests of capital in its phase of global conquest. At the same time, however, it created and reinforced rigid boundaries . . . that effectively blocked the free flow of capital, labor and goods – thus necessarily precluding the full realization of the world market.'[2] As capital realizes itself in the world market, it 'tends toward a smooth space defined by uncoded flows, flexibility, continual modulation, and tendential equalization'.[3]

The idea of Empire as a 'smooth space' is a central theme of the book. The smoothing does not just affect the division of the world into nation-states and their empires, merging and blending the distinct national colours 'in the imperial global rainbow'.[4] Most significant, it affects its division into First, Second and Third Worlds, North and South, core and periphery. While the Second World has disappeared, the Third World 'entered into the First, establishes itself at the heart as the ghetto, shanty town, favela'.[5] The First World, in turn, 'is tranferred to the Third in the form of stock exchanges and banks, transnational corporations and icy skyscrapers of money and command'.[6] As a result, 'center and periphery, North and South no longer define an international order but rather have moved closer to one another'.[7]

As in most accounts of globalization, Hardt and Negri trace its origins to the new power that the computer and information revolution has put in the hands of capital. By making it possible 'to link together different groups of labor in real time across the world', the revolution enabled capital 'to weaken the structural resistances of labor power' and 'to impose both temporal flexibility and spatial mobility'.[8] Speculative and financial capital strengthen the tendency by going 'where the price of labor is lowest and where the administrative force to guarantee exploitation is highest'.[9] As a result, 'the countries that still maintain the rigidities of labor and oppose its full flexibility and mobility are punished, tormented, and finally destroyed'.[10]

In contrast to most accounts of globalization, however, Hardt and Negri do not conceive of the forces of labour as the more or less reluctant recipients of the tendencies of capital. On the one hand, proletarian struggles 'caused directly' the capitalist crisis of the late 1960s and early 1970s, and thus 'forced capital to modify its own structures and undergo a paradigm shift'.[11]

If the Vietnam War had not taken place, if there had not been worker and student revolts in the 1960s, if there had not been 1968 and the second wave of the women's movements, if there had not been the whole series of anti-imperialist struggles, capital would have been content to maintain its own arrangement of power. . . . It would have been content for several good reasons: because the natural limits of development served it well; because it was threatened by the development of immaterial labor; because it knew that the transversal mobility and hybridization of world labor power opened the potential for new crises and class conflicts on an order never before experienced. The restructuring of production . . . was anticipated by the rise of a new subjectivity . . . was driven from below, by a proletariat whose composition had already changed.[12]

On the other hand, this new proletariat – or 'multitude', as Hardt and Negri call it – promptly seized the new opportunities of empowerment and liberation created by globalization. The key practice in this respect has been migration. 'The multitude's resistance to bondage – the struggle against the slavery of belonging to a nation, an identity, and a people, and thus the desertion from sovereignty and the limits it places on subjectivity – is entirely positive. . . . The real heroes of the liberation of the Third World today may really have been the emigrants and the flows of population that have destroyed old and new boundaries'.[13] The multitude is thus both protagonist and beneficiary of the destruction of boundaries that marks the coming of Empire.

Moreover, the very globalization of capital's networks of production and control empowers each and every point of revolt. Horizontal articulations among struggles – and hence the mediation of leaders, unions and parties – are no longer needed. 'Simply by focusing their own powers, concentrating their energies in a tense and compact coil . . . struggles strike directly at the highest articulations of imperial order'.[14]

As Hardt and Negri recognize, this double empowerment of the multitude under Empire leaves open the fundamental question of what kind of political programme can enable the multitude to cross and break down the limits that imperial initiatives continually re-establish on its desire of liberation. All they can say at this point is that global citizenship (*papiers pour tous!*) is a first element of such a programme, followed by a second element: a social wage and a guaranteed income for all individuals. 'Once [global] citizenship is extended to all, we could call this guaranteed income a citizenship income, due each as a member of [world] society.'[15]

This is probably the most optimistic picture of the nature and consequences of globalization proposed thus far by the radical left. The authors' endeavour to do away with any nostalgia for the power structures of an earlier era of capitalist development is, in my view, commendable. And so is their endeavour to show that the emerging logic and structure of world rule is both a response to past struggles of the exploited and oppressed and a more favourable terrain than previous structures for ongoing struggles against new forms of exploitation and oppression. There are, nonetheless, serious problems with the way Hardt and Negri pursue these commendable endeavours.

Most problems arise from Hardt and Negri's heavy reliance on metaphors and theories and systematic avoidance of empirical evidence. While many readers will undoubtedly be taken in by the erudition deployed throughout the book, more sceptical readers will be put off by statements of fact unbacked by empirical evidence or, worse still, easily falsifiable on the basis of widely available evidence. I will limit myself to two crucial examples, one concerning the 'smoothness' of the space of Empire, and the other concerning the role of the contemporary mobility of labour and capital in equalizing conditions of production and reproduction across that space.

It is hard to question that the disappearance of the Second World makes it anachronistic to continue to speak of a First and a Third World. There is also plenty of evidence that the signs of modernity associated with the wealth of the former First World (the 'icy skyscrapers of money and command') have proliferated in the former Third World; and it may also be the case that the signs of marginalization associated with the poverty of the former Third World are now more prominent in the former First World than they were twenty or thirty years ago. Nevertheless, it does not follow from all this that the distance between the poverty of the former Third World (or South) and the wealth of the former First World (or North) has decreased to any significant extent. Indeed, all available evidence shows an extraordinary persistence of the North–South income gap as measured by GNP per capita. Suffice it to mention that in 1999 the average per capita income of former 'Third World' countries was only 4.6 per cent of the per capita income of former 'First World' countries, that is, almost exactly what it was in 1960 (4.5 per cent) and in 1980 (4.3 per cent). Indeed, if we exclude China from the calculation, the percentage shows a steady decrease from 6.4 in 1960, to 6.0 in 1980 and 5.5 in 1999.[16]

Hardt and Negri's assertion of an ongoing supersession of the North–South divide is thus clearly false. Also flawed are their assertions concerning the direction and extent of contemporary flows of capital and labour. For one thing, they grossly exaggerate the extent to which these flows are unprecedented. This is especially true of their dismissal of nineteenth-century migrations as 'Lilliputian'[17] compared to their late twentieth-century counterparts. Proportionately speaking, nineteenth-century flows were in fact much larger, especially if we include migrations within and from Asia.[18] Moreover, the assertion that speculative and financial capital has been going 'where the price of labor is lowest and where the administrative force to guarantee exploitation is highest' is only in small part true. It is true, that is, only if we hold all kinds of other things equal, first and foremost per capita national income. But most other things (and especially per capita national income) are not at all equal among the world's regions and jurisdictions. As a result by far the largest share of capital flows is between wealthy countries (where the price of labour is comparatively high and the administrative force to guarantee exploitation comparatively low) with relatively little capital actually flowing from wealthy to poor countries.

These are not the only statements of fact in the narrative of *Empire* that, on close inspection, turn out to be false. They are, nonetheless, among the most crucial for the credibility not just of the book's reconstruction of present tendencies but for its political conclusions as well. For Hardt and Negri's optimism concerning the opportunities that globalization opens up for the liberation of the multitude largely rests on their assumption that capital under Empire tends towards a double equalization of the conditions of existence of the multitude: equalization through capital mobility from North to South and equalization through labour mobility from South to North. But if these mechanisms are not operative – as, for the time being, they do not appear to be – the road to global citizenship and to a guaranteed income for all citizens may be far longer, bumpier and more treacherous than Hardt and Negri would like us to believe.

II

I will deal with the possible configuration(s) of this bumpy and teacherous long march by responding to Hardt and Negri's criticism of my own account of the evolution of historical capitalism in early modern and modern times. Hardt and Negri include me among the authors who 'prepare[d] the terrain for the analysis and critique of Empire'.[19] At the same time, they single out my reconstruction of systemic cycles of accumulation in *The Long Twentieth Century* as an instance of cyclical theories of capitalism that obscure the novelty of contemporary transformations (*'from imperialism to Empire and from the nation-state to the political regulation of the global market'*)[20] as well as the driving force of those transformations (a '[c]lass struggle [that], pushing the nation-state towards its abolition and thus going beyond the barriers posed by it, proposes the constitution of Empire as the site of analysis and conflict').[21] More specifically, in their view.

> in the context of Arrighi's cyclical argument it is impossible to recognize a rupture of the system, a paradigm shift, an event. Instead, everything must always return, and the history of capitalism thus becomes the eternal return of the same. In the end such a cyclical analysis masks the motor of the process of crisis and restructuring. . . . [I]t seems that the crisis of the 1970s was simply part of the objective and inevitable cycles of capitalist accumulation, rather than the result of proletarian and anticapitalist attack both in the dominant and in the subordinated countries. The accumulation of these struggles was the motor of the crisis, and they determined the terms and nature of capitalist restructuring. . . . We have to recognize where in the transnational networks of production, the circuits of the world market, and the global structures of capitalist rule there is the potential for rupture and the motor for a future that is not simply doomed to repeat the past cycles of capitalism.[22]

I find this assessment curious for two reasons. One is that, for thirty years, I have been advancing a thesis about the crisis of the 1970s that, in many respects, resembles what, according to Hardt and Negri, *The Long Twentieth Century* obscures. And the other is that, although *The Long Twentieth Century* does construct cycles, its argument is not at all cyclical, nor does it contradict my earlier thesis about the crisis of the 1970s. It simply puts that thesis in a longer historical perspective. Let me deal with each of these two issues in turn.

In an article first published in Italian in 1972, I pointed out some crucial differences between the incipient capitalist crisis of the 1970s and the crises of 1873–96 and of the 1930s. The most important among these differences was the role of workers' struggles in precipitating the crisis of the 1970s. I further maintained that this and other differences meant that the incipient crisis was less likely than the earlier crises to result in an intensification of inter-imperialist rivalries and a consequent break up of the world market. Rather, the crisis could be expected to result in a strengthening of the unity of the world market and of the tendency towards the decentralization of industrial production towards capitalistically 'less developed' regions of the global economy.[23]

In *The Geometry of Imperialism*, published six years later, I carried this analysis one step further. Not only did I underscore again that the kind of world-economic integration via direct investment that had developed under US hegemony was less likely to break down in a generalized state of war among capitalist powers than the kind of world-economic integration via commodity and financial flows typical of nineteenth-century British hegemony, but, in addition, I pointed out that workers' struggles consolidated this new form of world-economic integration and suggested that, over time, the consolidation could be expected to weaken nation-states as the primary form of political organization of world capitalism.[24] It followed from this argument that the very theories of 'imperialism' that had been most successful in predicting trends in the first half of the twentieth century[25] had become hopelessly obsolete. These theories had become obsolete for the simple reason that world capitalism as instituted under US hegemony was no longer generating the tendency towards war among capitalist powers that constituted their specific *explanandum*. And, to the extent that the system of nation-states was actually ceasing to be the primary form of political organizations of world capitalism, the obsolescence of these theories would become permanent.[26]

Twelve years later[27] I recast these arguments in an account of the 'long' twentieth century that focused on the rise of the world labour movement in the late nineteenth century, the bifurcation of the movement into social-democratic and Marxist trajectories in the early twentieth century, the success of workers' struggles along both trajectories in provoking a fundamental, 'reformist' reorganization of world capitalism under US hegemony at the end of the Second World War, and the crisis that both kinds of movements faced in the 1980s as the unintended consequence of their previous successes. As in Hardt and Negri's similar story, I diagnosed this crisis – especially the crisis of Marxism as instituted in the first half of the twentieth century – as a positive rather than a negative development for the future of the world proletariat. Whereas Marxism had developed historically in a direction antithetical to the one foreseen and advocated by Marx, I argued, ongoing transformations of world capitalism – first and foremost the unprecedented degree of integration of the global market – were making Marx's predictions and prescriptions for the present and future of the world labour movement more rather than less relevant.

Starting from different premises and following a different line of argument, I thus reached conclusions very similar to one of the central theses of *Empire*. Unlike Hardt and Negri, I nonetheless qualified these conclusions with a warning against excessive confidence in the Marxian scheme of things.

> For in one major respect the Marxian scheme itself remains seriously defective – namely in the way in which it deals with the role of age, sex, race, nationality, religion and other natural and historical specificities in shaping the social identity of the world proletariat. . . . To be sure, the cost-cutting race of the [1970s and 1980s] has provided compelling evidence in support of [Marx's] observation that *for capital* all members of the proletariat are instruments of labour, more or less expensive to use according to their age, sex, colour, nationality, religion, etc. However, it has also shown that one cannot infer, as Marx does, from this predisposition of capital a predisposition of labour to relinquish natural and historical differences as means of affirming, individually and collectively, a distinctive social identity. Whenever faced with the predisposition of capital to treat labour as an undifferentiated mass with no individuality other than a differential capability to augment the value of capital, proletarians have rebelled. Almost invariably they have seized upon or created anew whatever combination of distinctive traits (age, sex, colour, assorted geo-historical specificities) they could use to impose on capital some kind of

special treatment. As a consequence, patriarchalism, racism and
national-chauvinism have been integral to the making of the world
labour movement along both trajectories, and live on in one form or
another in most proletarian ideologies and organisations.[28]

Even before completing *The Long Twentieth Century*, I was thus far
less sanguine than Hardt and Negri about the possibility that
under the emerging condition of world-market integration, proletarian 'exit' (South–North migrations) and 'voice' (struggles
against exploitation, exclusion and oppression) would promote
greater solidarity, equality and democracy across national, civili-
zational, racial and gender divides. It seems to me that the 1990s
have provided plenty of evidence both against the idealized and
idealistic view of the multitude that Hardt and Negri advance in
Empire, and in favour of my earlier warning that intensifying
competition in the global market – including and especially
intensification through labour migration – could well strengthen
the patriarchalist, racist and national-chauvinist dispositions of
the world proletariat. This is a first important reason why in my
view the road to global citizenship and to a guaranteed income
for all citizens can be expected to be far longer, bumpier and
more treacherous than Hardt and Negri maintain.

Other equally important reasons have to do with Hardt and
Negri's idealized and idealistic view, not just of the multitude, but
of capital and Empire as well. It is in this connection that their
misreading of my reconstruction of systemic cycles of accumulation
becomes relevant. For the reconstruction neither prevents a recognition of systemic ruptures and paradigm shifts, nor describes
the history of capitalism as an eternal return of the same, nor
masks the motor of the process of crisis and restructuring, as Hardt
and Negri maintain. Indeed, it does exactly the opposite by showing that, world-historically, systemic ruptures and paradigm shifts
occur precisely when the 'same' (in the form of recurrent system-
wide financial expansions) appears to (and in a sense actually
does) return. Moreover, by comparing successive periods of
return/rupture, it shows how the motor of crisis and restructuring
(as well as the agency of capitalist expansion) has changed over
time, making the present crisis novel in key respects.

More specifically, the reconstruction of systemic cycles of accumulation serves a double purpose. First, it serves the purpose of

identifying the distinguishing features of world capitalism as a
historical (as opposed to an ideal-typical) social system. And second, it serves the purpose of identifying what is truly new in the
present condition of world capitalism in the light of its entire life
history, as opposed to what may appear new in the light of some
temporally or spatially partial view of that history. It seems to me
that these two identifications are essential to a historically
grounded recognition – to paraphrase Hardt and Negri's previously quoted passage – of where in the global structures of
capitalist rule there is the potential for rupture and the motor for
a future that is not simply doomed to repeat the past cycles of
capitalism. Such a historically grounded recognition does not so
much contradict (though in part it does) as add important new
dimensions to my earlier – and Hardt and Negri's present –
assessment of the emergent condition of world rule. Let me
briefly mention the most important of these new dimensions.

First, while confirming the plausibility of the contention that a
world state (which I have no objections to calling 'Empire') is in
formation, my reconstruction of systemic cycles of accumulation
adds both a temporal scale and an element of uncertainty to the
ongoing transition from a phase of world history based on
national states to a possible but by no means certain world-state
phase. As *The Long Twentieth Century* and subsequent work on
hegemonic transitions show, world capitalism was originally
embedded in a system of city-states and the transition from the
city-state phase to the nation-state phase of capitalism stretched
over several centuries. For at least two centuries of this transition,
city-states (most notably Venice) or business diasporas originating
in city-states (most notably the Genoese) remained protagonists
of the capitalist dynamic, while the leading agency of the transition itself was a state (the United Provinces) that combined
characteristics of the declining city-states and of the rising nation-
states.[29] Although we also noted a certain acceleration in the pace
of world-systemic transformations, past experience seems to suggest
that the present transition from the nation-state to a world-state
phase of world rule will take at least a century to complete. It also
suggests that at least some national states or hybrid forms of
nation- and world-state may be protagonists of the transition.

Second, much of the uncertainty surrounding ongoing transformations derives from the fact that past periods of financial

expansion and hegemonic transition have been moments of increasing instability and unintended capitalist self-destructiveness. Although a major factor of past instability and self-destructiveness (inter-imperialist wars) is unlikely to intervene, the attempt of today's declining hegemonic power (the United States) to impose on the world an exploitative domination may well become a more important source of instability and self-destructiveness than similar attempts by its predecessors.[30] Thus, paraphrasing Joseph Schumpeter,[31] *The Long Twentieth Century* concluded that 'before humanity chokes (or basks) in the dungeon (or paradise) of a post-capitalist world empire or of a post-capitalist world market society, it may well burn up in the horrors (or glories) of the escalating violence that has accompanied the liquidation of the Cold War world order'.[32]

Third, a comparison of the present with past transitions does confirm the historically novel role that proletarian and anticapitalist struggles, both in the dominant and subordinate countries, have played in precipitating the crisis of the 1970s. Indeed, in a very real sense the present financial expansion (unlike previous similar expansions) has been primarily an instrument – to paraphrase Immanuel Wallerstein[33] – of the containment of the combined demands of the peoples of the non-Western world (for relatively little per person but for a lot of people) and of the Western working classes (for relatively few people but for quite a lot per person). At the same time, however, the financial expansion and associated restructuring of the global political economy have had considerable success in disorganizing the social forces that were the bearers of these demands in the upheavals of the late 1960s and 1970s. Integral to this success has been the reproduction of the North–South income divide which, as previously noted, is as large today as it was twenty or forty years ago. It is hard to believe that this huge and persistent divide will not continue to play a decisive role in shaping, not just proletarian identities and dispositions North and South, but also processes of world-state formation. As the implosion of the World Trade Organization talks in Seattle has shown in exemplary fashion, the struggle over the social orientation of the emerging world-state is as much a struggle between North and South as it is between capital and labour. Indeed, since the possessors of capital continue to be overwhelmingly concentrated in the North, while a vast and ever-growing majority of the world's proletariat is concentrated in the South, the two struggles are in good part obverse sides of the same coin.[34]

Finally, while the overall North–South divide has remained remarkably stable, over the last forty years there has been a major relocation of manufacturing activities and world market shares from North America and Western Europe to East Asia. Thus, between 1960 and 1999, the East Asian share of world value added (a good measure of the share of the world market controlled by the residents of the region) increased from 13 per cent to 25.9 per cent, while the North American share decreased from 35.2 per cent to 29.8 per cent and the Western European share decreased from 40.5 per cent to 32.3 per cent. Even more significant was the shift in the shares of world value added in manufacturing, with the East Asian share increasing in the same period from 16.4 per cent to 35.2 per cent, against a decrease in the North American share from 42.2 per cent to 29.9 per cent and of the Western European share from 32.4 per cent to 23.4 per cent.[35] It is hardly plausible that shifts of this order will not affect the constitution of Empire, particularly in view of the fact that East Asia has a much longer history of state and market formation than Europe and North America.[36] And yet, Hardt and Negri focus exclusively on the Euro-American lineages of Empire and do not even entertain the possibility of their hybridization with Asian lineages.

In short, Empire may indeed to be in the making, but, if it is, it may well take a century or more before humanity will know whether its constitution has succeeded or failed, and, if it has succeeded, what its social and cultural contents will be. In the meantime, all we can hope for is that the ruling classes of the declining and rising centres of the global economy deploy in their actions a greater intelligence than they have done so far; that proletarian struggles shun patriarchalist, racist and national-chauvinistic temptations; and that activists and intellectuals of good will develop a better understanding of where Empire is coming from and where it can and cannot go.

Notes

1. Michael Hardt and Antonio Negri *Empire*, Cambridge, MA: Harvard University Press 2000, p. 332.
2. Ibid., p. 332.
3. Ibid., p. 327.
4. Ibid., p. xiii.
5. Ibid., p. 254.
6. Ibid., p. 254.
7. Ibid., p. 336.
8. Ibid., p. 327.
9. Ibid., p. 338.
10. Ibid., pp. 337–8.
11. Ibid., p. 261.
12. Ibid., pp. 275–6.
13. Ibid., pp. 361–3.
14. Ibid., p. 58.
15. Ibid., p. 403.
16. All figures calculated from World Bank, *World Tables*, vols 1 and 2, Washington: World Bank 1984; and World Bank, *World Development Indicators*, CD-ROM, Washington: World Bank 2001.
17. *Empire*, p. 213.
18. David Held, Anthony McGrew, David Goldblatt and Jonathan Perraton, *Global Transformations*, Stanford: Stanford University Press 1999, chapter 6.
19. *Empire*, p. 415.
20. Ibid., p. 237; italics in original.
21. Ibid., p. 237.
22. Ibid., p. 239; italics in original.
23. Giovanni Arrighi, 'Towards a Theory of Capitalist Crisis', *New Left Review*, I/III (1978), pp. 3–24.
24. Giovanni Arrighi, *The Geometry of Imperialism: The Limits of Hobson's Paradigm* (2nd edn), London: Verso 1983, pp. 146–8.
25. Most notably, John Hobson, *Imperialism: A Study*, London: George Allen & Unwin 1938; Rudolf Hilferding, *Finance Capital: A Study of the Latest Phase of Capitalist Development*, London: Routledge 1981; Vladimir Lenin, *Imperialism: The Highest Stage of Capitalism*, in *Selected Works*, vol. 1, Moscow: Foreign Languages Publishing House 1952.
26. Arrighi, *The Geometry of Imperialism*, pp. 149–73.
27. Giovanni Arrighi, 'Marxist Century, American Century. The Making and Remaking of the World Labour Movement', *New Left Review*, 1/179 (1990), pp. 29–63.
28. Arrighi, 'Marxist Century, American Century', p. 63; emphasis in original.
29. Giovanni Arrighi, *The Long Twentieth Century: Money, Power and the Origins of Our Time*, London: Verso 1993, pp. 11, 36–47 and 82–158; and Giovanni Arrighi and Beverly Silver, *Chaos and Governance in the Modern World System*, Minneapolis: University of Minnesota Press 1999, pp. 37–58.
30. Giovanni Arrighi and Beverly Silver, 'Capitalism and World (Dis)order', *Review of International Studies*, 27 (2001), pp. 257–79.

31. Joseph Schumpeter, *Capitalism, Socialism and Democracy*, London: George Allen & Unwin 1954, p. 163.

32. *The Long Twentieth Century*, p. 356.

33. Immanuel Wallerstein, 'Response: Declining States, Declining Rights?', *International Labor and Working-Class History*, 47 (1995), pp. 24–7.

34. 'Capitalism and World (Dis)order' and Beverly Silver, *Forces of Labour: Workers' Movements and Globalisation since 1870*, Cambridge: Cambridge University Press (forthcoming).

35. All percentages calculated from World Bank, 1984 and 2001.

36. *Chaos and Governance in the Modern World System*, chapter 4.

5

Back to the Future?

Sanjay Seth

There was a time when the energies of the left were wholly invested in envisioning and bringing into being a new social order in which differences such as those of class, race and gender were either effaced or rendered irrelevant. For some time now, however, the more interesting intellectual debates have been concerned with 'difference' – with the ethical imperative to recognize and attend to it rather than subsume it, and with modernity and Enlightenment, which can be seen as having ignored or sought to efface it. Hardt and Negri argue that certain dramatic social changes mean that our relation to this concern should also be changing. For these authors the logic of globalization is not only inexorable, and desirable – the forward march of capitalism in the form of a deterritorialized global empire also leads to the possibilities of an intensified resistance by the proletariat, here redesignated as the 'multitude'. The endpoint is a cosmopolitan communism not unlike that envisioned by Marx. Theories such as postcolonialism and postmodernism, concerned with deconstructing the binary logic through which the modern is thought and lived, are tilting at windmills, for the new capitalism which has developed, itself deconstructs binaries, just as it dissolves territories and all fixity.

Hardt and Negri are indebted to Marx as well as others (perhaps most notably Deleuze[1]), but their departures from Marxism are also extensive, and these aspects of their analysis will not find favour among more orthodox Marxists. Nonetheless, the general (dialectical) tenor of their argument remains deeply indebted to the Marxist tradition. Just as Lenin's amendments to Marx's theory were justified by arguing that such revisions were occasioned by a change in the nature of capitalism, so Hardt and Negri anchor their theoretical innovations mainly on the fact that the object of analysis has changed. For Lenin the transmutation of capitalism into monopoly capitalism led to the phenomenon of imperialism (and the need for a concept to capture and render this new reality); for Hardt and Negri imperialism in turn has been rendered redundant – 'it eventually became a fetter to the deterritorializing flows and smooth space of capitalist development, and ultimately it had to be cast aside'[2] and replaced by Empire. Both the analysis and the language deliberately signal the influence of Marx.

The rhythms and dynamic of their analysis also mirror the form, though not always the content, of Marx's argument. Marx, as all know, welcomed capitalism as a historically progressive form; Hardt and Negri similarly proclaim that Empire, for all its inequities, is to be welcomed: 'We claim that Empire is better in the same way that Marx insists that capitalism is better than the forms of society and modes of production that came before it. Marx's view is grounded on a healthy and lucid disgust for the parochial and rigid hierarchies that preceded capitalist society as well as on a recognition that the potential for liberation is increased in the new situation.'[3]

The development of Empire means that the struggle against it is raised to a new and global terrain, free of the petty nationalisms and localisms which characterized (and all too often derailed) anti-capitalist struggle before. The 'multitude', that expanded notion of the proletariat ('a broad category that includes all those whose labor is directly or indirectly exploited by and subjected to capitalist norms of production and reproduction'),[4] is driven to a struggle against Empire on a global terrain for an end to all forms of exploitation. A new form of solidarity and militancy is visible, according to Hardt and Negri, in struggles as diverse as those of Chinese students in Tiananmen Square, as the Intifada, the struggles in the Chiapas, 'race riots' in Los Angeles, and so on. They register the fact that these struggles do not in fact communicate with each other, that they don't seem to direct themselves against a common enemy and that the language in which they struggle is usually not that of socialism. Despite this, such struggles, write Hardt and Negri, 'directly attack the global order of Empire and seek a real alternative',[5] and for this reason *Empire* ends by expressing optimism that the multitude will succeed in becoming a revolutionary political subject. All indications are that the struggles they name are unconnected, and sometimes not very radical; but this turns out to be a virtue, for their very localness and inability to link up horizontally means that they 'leap immediately to the global level and attack the imperial constitution in its generality'.[6] There *are* some signs of the coalescence of diverse struggles on a world scale, such as during the Seattle protests, and Hardt and Negri may yet be proven right. But here their argument is not carried by the weight of evidence but rather by the momentum of their dialectic.

In the passage quoted above Hardt and Negri declare, citing Marx as their precedent, that globalization is to be welcomed, both because it is better than narrow parochialisms, and because it provides the foundations for the leap into a qualitatively better society. They elaborate that the European 'discovery' and colonization of the world, bloody and barbaric as it was, also contained a utopian element and possibility. Again, Marx is one of the examples of this utopian aspect (Bartolomé de Las Casas and Toussaint L'Ouverture are the other two).[7] When in 1853 Marx wrote a series of articles on India for the *New York Daily Tribune*, he denounced the hypocrisy and greed of the British, which had undermined the traditional Indian village community and caused great suffering.[8] However, it was important not to forget, wrote Marx, that these village communities 'had always been the solid foundation of Oriental despotism, that they restrained the human mind, within the smallest possible compass, making it the unresisting tool of superstition, enslaving it beneath the traditional rules depriving it of all grandeur and historical energies'.[9] In destroying this and 'laying the material foundations of Western society in Asia' British colonialism, despite its crimes, 'was the unconscious tool of history'. Hardt and Negri rebuke Marx for assuming that Westernization is the only possible alternative to traditional social forms, but otherwise they cite him approvingly for seeing the utopian possibilities in the globalization of his day. A similar recognition, they declare, 'is what prevents us from simply falling back into particularism and isolationism . . . pushing us instead to forge a project of counterglobalisation'.[10]

It was on grounds such as these that the liberals and socialists who were the inheritors of the Enlightenment could champion the globalization of liberty, autonomy and reason, confident that these were superior to constraint and superstition. To the degree that the globalization of Europe could be seen as the bearer of these values, it too could be welcomed; or if it at least laid their foundations, it could be welcomed in a qualified fashion, as the 'unconscious tool of history'; or else it could be denounced for *failing* to deliver ('colonialism retards development, hence must be overthrown'), and the better order embodied in Western modernity pursued under the sign of nationalism or socialism.

It has been one of the fruits of postmodernism and postcolonialism, it seems to me, that both these arguments are harder to make today than they were even a few decades ago.[11] Hardt and Negri draw upon Hegel and Marx – theirs is a full-fledged dialectic (although they are deeply uncomfortable with this, and deny it), the telos of which is universal freedom in the form of socialism. They are by no means indifferent to the claims of difference, but they doubt that theories which accord centrality to difference are useful, because, they suggest, difference in any case no longer means what it did. Contemporary capitalism produces in equal measure the global and the local, and thus 'It is false . . . to claim that we can (re)establish local identities that are in some sense *outside* and protected against the global flows of capital and Empire'.[12] There is no 'non-West', no Third World, for these are themselves the effect of the global machine, and thus offer no licence for an ethical or political project which might counterpose them to the universal and the global. And theories which have emphasized the binary nature of modern and colonial thought and sought to deconstruct and dismantle it, such as postmodernism and postcolonialism, are fighting a disappearing target: 'the postmodernist and postcolonial theories who advocate a politics of difference . . . have been outflanked by the [new, global] strategies of power. Power has evacuated the bastion they are attacking and has circled around to the rear to join them in the assault in the name of difference.'[13]

This is an interesting argument (as is the claim that postcolonialism is in any case an effect of globalization, a point I will return to at the end of this essay) but it conceals a conceptual slide. This lies in the word 'modern', or rather the relation posited between this and Europe. Hardt and Negri write that they begin their story in Europe and North America, not because they wish to privilege it, but because this is where Empire and the concepts and practices which characterize it first developed. But, they add, '[w]hereas the genealogy of Empire is in this sense Eurocentric . . . its present powers are not limited to any region'.[14] Compare this with the following statement by Hedley Bull and Adam Watson, explaining that they treat the originally European system of state relations as a global system not because of any Western arrogance on their part, but because what was once Eurocentric is now global: 'It is not our perspective but the historical record itself that can be called Eurocentric.'[15] I counterpose this to Hardt and Negri not to suggest some fundamental convergence between their arguments and those of two relatively conservative international relations theorists, but rather to show that there is a widely used intellectual 'move' which allows one to argue that, in becoming global, what was once the *European*-modern ceased being specifically (and in that sense parochially) European. Now, if it were true that not a trace of other worlds was left – if there was not a trace of a subject who was not a bourgeois self, possessed of interiority and the desire for autonomy, no form of community that was not representable as a nation and governable by a state – then there might be no vantage point from which we could speak of (radical) difference. 'Europe' would be coextensive with the world, and we would all be variations on the 'modern'.

But the triumph of the social transformations we label modern, which began in Europe some centuries ago and have since undoubtedly transformed the rest of the world, has not been that complete. To say this is not to be guilty of a nostalgic and ill-conceived hankering for a non-existent point 'outside' Empire and the modern. It is rather to suggest that, even where everything *has* become part of a capitalist system, this does not establish equivalence between the different moments and elements of what can still be seen as a single system. It was one of Lenin's insights (drawing on Marx), not yet rendered irrelevant, that the expansion of capital can occur without necessarily refashioning in its own image the new areas/processes which it subordinates; that there can be uneven development in which a 'formal' subsumption to capital is not accompanied by a 'real' subsumption.

To make the point in this way is still to engage in an argument about the character and extent of capitalist globalization, an argument which (in principle, at least) is resolvable in empirical terms. Even if the process of capitalist expansion is so complete that there is no 'outside' of globalization, I have argued that it does not follow that any project which would challenge its universalizing imperative is quixotic or, worse, nostalgically reactionary. I made this argument in terms of the continued existence of forms of life and knowledge which, even if they have been incorporated into global capitalism, have not been remade in its image. I want to stick to this argument, but also acknowledge that it lends itself all too readily to the historicist language of 'survivals', and thus immediately raises the question of how long these survivals will continue to survive. It could also be read as suggesting that postcolonial theory, in the name of which I have made a case for continuing to be attentive to difference, somehow 'represents' these survivals, even speaks for a subaltern figure such as the peasant. But that is not at all what I wish to suggest.

When Hardt and Negri suggest that postcolonialism is in an important sense an effect of globalization (pp. 138–9), I think they are profoundly right, although not perhaps quite in the sense that they intend. It is only when capitalism has extended its sway to the point where little or nothing lies outside it that we can see a difference which exists in the interstices of capital, a moment which is in the life of capital but not entirely of it. It is to these differences – not necessarily or only 'pre-capitalist' – that postcolonialism attends, and in this sense it too is only possible after capitalism has colonized the world, when there is no 'outside' from which and in the name of which to criticize.

Let me clarify this point by drawing on Dipesh Chakrabarty's *Provincializing Europe: Postcolonial Thought and Historical Difference.* Reading Marx somewhat against the grain, Chakrabarty suggests that, for Marx, once capital has fully developed, there are certain historical transformations (e.g. the separation of labour from the land) which appear, retrospectively, as the logical presuppositions of capital. That is, once one has grasped the structure of capital (which can only be done retrospectively, when capital is triumphant and its structure clear), one can see that certain historical events are a necessary part of its emergence, are posited by capital as the conditions for its own emergence (the positing is done not by history, which would be a very teleological account indeed, but as a perspective from which the *logically* necessary conditions for the emergence of capitalism can be seen to have also *historically* occurred). But there are other elements of the past, which capitalism also encounters as antecedents to it, but – Chakrabarty quotes Marx – 'not as antecedents established by itself, not as forms of its own life-process'.[16] These are pasts which are not 'outside' capital, but nor are they logical preconditions of it, *necessary* elements in the history of capital. In other words, Marx accepts, according to Chakrabarty, 'that the total universe of pasts that capital encounters is larger than the sum of those in which are worked out the logical presuppositions of capital'.[17] These other pasts may be part of the 'precapitalist' past of a society, but they also may not, consisting instead of structures of affect which might (or might not) coexist with capital, but are not part of the world it posits.

If this is true, then globalization can never be the same as the universalization of capital.[18] Globalization will never remake the world for capital, for structures of affect and multiple ways of being human which are not part of the necessary history and structure of capital continue to inhere in capital, even where it has done its work of transformation most thoroughly. Difference continues to exist, although 'Difference, in this account, is not something external to capital. Nor is it something subsumed into capital. It lives in intimate and plural relations to capital, ranging from opposition to neutrality.'[19]

It is in this spirit that I dissent from the suggestion that difference itself is now created by Empire and the market, and therefore that the time when it was ethically important to attend to difference is passing. We still need, it seems to me, to be attentive to difference, and to work our way 'through' difference, rather than to surpass it. Postcolonialism is still a useful tool in that enterprise, not as the voice of the premodern subaltern, but rather as that which keeps us sensitive to what is in but not of capital. Like the difference to which it attends postcolonialism does not lie outside the belly of the best, but it has not been digested by it, and it has functions still to fulfil, for it is too soon to 'go back to the future'.

Notes

1. Hardt is the author of *Gilles Deleuze: An Apprenticeship in Philosophy*, London: UCL Press 1993.
2. Michael Hardt and Antonio Negri, *Empire*, Cambridge, MA: Harvard University Press 2000, p. 333.
3. Ibid., p. 43.
4. Ibid., p. 52.
5. Ibid., pp. 56–7.
6. Ibid., p. 56.
7. Toussaint L'Ouverture was the leader of a slave revolt in Haiti, the subject of C. L. R. James' classic *The Black Jacobins*, New York: Vintage Books 1963. Las Casas was the sixteenth-century Spanish priest who argued that the Amerindians were, after all, men, and that the Spanish treatment of them was unconscionable. See Lewis Hanke, *Aristotle and the American Indians*, Chicago, IL: Regency 1959.
8. Marx's understanding of the village community as an autarchic little republic was based upon a series of colonial reports, which in turn bore only passing resemblance to rural life in colonial India. See L. Dumont, 'The "village community" from Munro to Maine', *Contributions to Indian Sociology*, IX 1966.
9. *Empire*, p. 119.
10. Ibid., p. 115.
11. And when they are made, as of course they continue to be, they occur in full awareness of the fact that it cannot simply be assumed that autonomy and the like are supra-cultural moral truths. For example, while John Rawls and Jürgen Habermas seek to retrieve the Kantian answer (but without the metaphysics), they also acknowledge that Reason never is 'pure', but that it is deeply rooted in a particular moral and philosophical tradition. In Rawls' later works he abandons altogether the claim that autonomy and equality are values for which a culture-free sanction can be found. See, for instance, *Political Liberalism*, New York: Columbia University Press, 1993. For a critique, see Sanjay Seth, 'Liberalism and the politics of (multi)culture: or, plurality is not difference', *Postcolonial Studies*, 4(1) 2001, pp. 65–77.
12. *Empire*, p. 45.
13. Ibid., p. 138.
14. Ibid., p. xvi.
15. Hedley Bull and Adam Watson, 'Introduction', in Bull and Watson (eds), *The Expansion of International Society*, Oxford: Oxford University Press 1984, p. 2.
16. Chakrabarty, *Provincializing Europe: Postcolonial Thought and Historical Difference*, Princeton, NJ: Princeton University Press 2000, p. 63.
17. Ibid., p. 64.
18. In a recent review of Chakrabarty's book, Hardt describes the difference between his and Chakrabarty's view on this point thus: 'My formulation would lead to the conception of . . . a strong contemporaneity [between a 'third world' society and a first world one] that contains within it differences and multiplicities. Chakrabarty's formulation instead leads to a conception of multiple, incommensurable times that exist simultaneously.' Hardt added that

'these two formulations may not be as different as they initially appear', but I suggest that Hardt's own way of framing the difference reveals how significant it is. See Hardt, 'The Eurocentricism of History', *Postcolonial Studies*, 4(2), 2000, pp. 243–9.

19. Chakrabarty, *Provincializing Europe*, p. 66.

6

Gems and Baubles in *Empire*

Leo Panitch and Sam Gindin

For an often indecipherable book with openly revolutionary aspirations, Hardt and Negri's *Empire* has received an astonishing degree of mainstream, as well as radical, attention.[1] This in itself suggests the need for a serious investigation of *Empire*'s content, but our interest does not lie in identifying this book as a curious cultural artefact. *Empire* is ultimately an important book because serious engagement with the contradictory richness of its ideas on the nature of Empire, capitalism and resistance in our time can help advance the 'liberatory' project that we share with Hardt and Negri. Only the most ungenerous of reviewers could fail to admire the ambitious scope of their attempt to integrate history, philosophy, sociology, culture, and economics *with* a politics from below. And, yet, the end result is a most frustrating book: full of promise but also of inconsistencies, self-contradictions, flights of exaggeration, and gaps in logic.

Empire's primary analytical goal, like that of so many recent books on globalization, is to explain the genesis and nature of a new type of capitalist order that 'rules over the entire "civilized" world.'[2] In this new global capitalist empire, nation-states (including the former imperialist powers themselves) and the internal power relations within them are 'penetrated' by a 'new sovereign, supranational world power', so that 'the conflict and competition among several imperial powers has in important respects been replaced by the idea of a single power that overdetermines them all, structures them in a unitary way, and treats them under one common notion of right that is decidedly postcolonial and postimperialist.'[3]

The essence of Hardt and Negri's argument takes shape in the form of a panorama of the passage from modernity to postmodernity. Modernity is presented as the process of secularization that, like all else in history since the medieval era, stemmed from the 'reappropriation' by 'the multitude' (a term they seem to derive from William of Occam – 'Ecclesia est multitudo fidelium') of its 'liberatory' potential.[4] After the old order was toppled by the allegedly unmediated and spontaneous power of the multitude, however, the revolution of modernity met a generalized 'Thermidor' which resulted in the multitude's reconstruction as the 'people' of the nation-state – 'a transcendent apparatus that could impose order on the multitude and prevent it from organizing itself spontaneously and expressing its creativity autonomously'.[5] The development of the modern conception of sovereignty reaches its 'counterrevolutionary' culmination in Hegel's political philosophy in which the liberation of modern humanity can only be a function of domination, that 'the immanent goal of the multitude is transformed into the necessary and transcendent power of the state'. This is, however, 'inseparable from capitalism': 'Modern European sovereignty is capitalist sovereignty, a form of command that overdetermines the relationship between individuality and universality as a function of the development of capital.'[6] The transition from agriculture to industry, followed by the diffusion of industrialization's cultural rhythms and the inability of the new proletariat to consume all that is produced at home, sets in train the dynamics that push European states to extend their sovereignty into other social formations – i.e. to become imperialist states.

It was, according to Hardt and Negri, the collapse of imperialism after World War Two and the American state's global generalization of its New Deal response to the Great Depression, that set the stage for postmodernity. But, here again, it was the multitude's spontaneous assertion of its search for unmediated 'liberatory' power in the 1960s (exemplified by rank-and-file worker rebellions, new social movements and postcolonial revolts) that determined the unfolding of the post-imperialist world. It was replaced by 'Empire' expressing the decentred and expansive 'network power' that American state sovereignty had been uniquely founded on in the modern era. This new non-imperialist 'Empire' emerged in response to the revolt from

below, transcending the multitude's spontaneous drive for freedom by means of a new 'flexible' disciplinary apparatus of order
'beyond borders'. This was founded on an aggressive attack,
following on the capitalist crisis of the early 1970s, on all barriers
to capital accumulation, transforming the nature of production
and surplus creation, and finally pushing the nation-state off the
stage of history.

This panorama of the history of the world from modernity to
postmodernity rests primarily on a series of interrelated and
problematic stories that Hardt and Negri tell about the multitude's contradictory relation to state sovereignty and the culmination of its historical evolution into the virtual rule of 'Empire'.
Hardt and Negri are adamant throughout, however, that every
story needs a material foundation. For all its twists and turns, the
political, cultural and metaphysical roller-coaster of narratives
Hardt and Negri take us on keeps trying to return to the world of
production and political economy, where the multitude takes
shape for them as 'the proletariat'. With an explicit bow in their
Preface to Marx's own decisive descent 'into the hidden abode of
production',[7] Hardt and Negri insist that their concept of Empire
as a new order would 'be merely a hollow husk if we were not to
designate also a new régime of *production*'.[8] And it is also in the
'realm of production . . . where the most effective resistances and
alternatives to the power of Empire arise'.[9] Thus, even though
they only get to any sustained attempt at a political economy after
page 200 of the book, it is here that any serious review of *Empire*
must properly begin.

The political economy of Empire:
the immateriality of immaterial production

What we are offered is an analysis that narrows its focus to the
workplace and tends to a crude technological determinism. The
economic contradictions of Empire are now directly located in
the sphere of production, in the technological and institutional
changes summarized in 'informatization' of the communications
revolution and in the allegedly new workforce that is the result.
The new jobs are 'highly mobile and involve flexible skills'. They
are generally characterized 'by the central role played by knowledge, information, affect, and communication'.[10] This marks a

'new mode of becoming human',[11] and it is now only the revolutionary subjectivity that this suggests that threatens systemic stability.

Hardt and Negri begin with the impact of informatization on the 'old' industrial sectors. This is a constructive starting point. The left has too casually written off the dynamism of capitalism by arguing that the traditional industrial sectors are in terminal decline, while the 'new economy' is isolated to particular spheres. What has given American capitalism in particular the material base for its expanded reproduction (materially and culturally) today is in large part the dissemination of the new technology *throughout* the economy – not as an independent force but in the context of other managerial strategies driven by competition and class conflict. In the auto industry, for example, the new information technology is playing a critical role in transforming the processes of design and tooling, of accounting and co-ordination, of outsourcing and 'just-in-time' supplier relations, of in-plant processes and worker roles and of the links between production and consumption.

But it is in the service sector that Hardt and Negri really want to locate the most dramatic transformation of production, including, above all, the new 'immaterial labour of analytical and symbolic tasks' and the 'production and manipulation of affects [that] requires human contact'.[12] It is necessary to pose the question of whether the record of the three decades since these trends began really does suggest a radically new militancy and new consciousness in the 'new' working class, and whether this sustains the strategic considerations for revolution that Hardt and Negri entertain.

The theory of revolution against Empire: a multitude of evasions

This vision of material history leads to a peculiar valorization of the American working class. The case for this is especially made in one startling passage amidst their account of the rise of Empire[13] where they insist on pretending that this new world order is actually determined by the 'power and creativity of the US proletariat' which allegedly 'expresses most fully the desires and needs of international or multinational workers'. Rather than being seen, as is conventionally thought, as 'weak' because of its 'low party and union representation', Hardt and Negri, in a wildly exaggerated fashion even for the autonomists they are, see the US working class as 'strong' for this very reason, somehow imagining that the great virtue of workers remaining or becoming unorganized ('inside' as well as 'outside the factories') allows them to exhibit the greatest degree of 'conflictuality', thereby posing 'serious threats and creative alternatives'.

We normally applaud efforts to make class struggle central to any analysis of capitalism's development (and Hardt and Negri's attempt to incorporate this is at least a welcome antidote to Robert Brenner's recent work, even if they at the same time go to the other extreme and merely ignore the significance of capitalist competition at the centre of his analysis).[14] But the unmediated power they want to ascribe to the contemporary American proletariat, and with and through it to the world's multitudes, just will not sustain any serious scrutiny, nor does it take us very far in developing adequate revolutionary strategies. There is simply no place to root any serious transformative politics in a world made up of a virtual Empire and a virtual proletariat.

What is this virtual proletariat? We can agree with their definition that takes the working class beyond traditional industrial workers and beyond the world of work itself (although both of these amendments are by now hardly anything novel), and we applaud their concern to locate a new strategic core among the broad proletariat. But can we really credit in this respect the new resistance and new confidence that Hardt and Negri find inherent in the new information and service workers? Do they know new things, have more control over their workplace, relate to each other differently, come to work with different expectations, go home with different dreams? Do they necessarily see their clients as potential allies, does the experience necessarily produce a new sense of collectivity? Is their work inherently more social than the social co-operation involved in the production of goods? Or, as with the industrial proletariat, is their humanity cramped by the context in which technology mediates human interaction *unless and until* they begin to discover through struggle, their own potentials as agency?

There are even more problems in the way they vaguely connect this strategic core of the proletariat to the 'multitude' today.

Included in both terms are very broad categories of oppression
(gender, race, ethno-national and so on), but what especially
characterizes the latter is 'the new mobility and hybridity of
subjects', where 'nomadism and miscegenation appear here as
subjects of virtue', and where the 'power to circulate' across
borders is 'the most creative force' for liberation today.[15] They
are right to ask where 'the great innovative sectors of immaterial
production, from design to fashion, and from electronics to
science [would] be without the "illegal labour" of the great
masses, mobilized towards the radiant horizons of capitalist wealth
and freedom'. But what makes them more revolutionary than
previous generations of immigrants? Does their desire for liberation, which is indeed real enough after all the suffering and
defeats that impels this migration, itself allow for them to
'reappropriate new spaces, around which are constructed new
freedoms . . . new forms of life and co-operation' nearly as autonomously of the state and capital as Hardt and Negri suggest? Are
they any less susceptible to becoming prisoners of the American
dream? Having vastly overstated what has already been demonstrated by the multitude in this respect, they suddenly become
rather more sober:

> Recognizing the potential autonomy of the mobile multitude, how-
> ever, only points towards the real question. What we need to grasp is
> how the multitude is organized and redefined as a positive, political
> power. . . . This leads us back to the fundamental questions: How can
> the actions of the multitude become political? How can the multitude
> organize and concentrate its energies against the repression and
> incessant territorial segmentations of Empire?[16]

This is indeed the right set of questions, yet, when Hardt and
Negri ask 'what specific and concrete task will animate this
political project?',[17] what they reply is telling. They admit that the
way they pose the question 'remains rather abstract' and admit
they 'cannot say at this point' what 'specific and concrete practices
will animate this project'.[18] Instead, they conclude by putting
forward a programme with three central political demands: global
citizenship, a guaranteed annual income, and the right to reappropriation. The first of these, 'global citizenship', essentially
involves the universalization of the liberal equality promised
within the nation-state. The second demand does turn to the

issue of how to achieve the substantive social right to equality of condition within liberalism – a social wage and guaranteed minimum income for all. But if this is an advance on liberalism, it remains solidly within the social-democratic tradition of focusing on the terrain of distribution rather than the social relations of production.

And so we come to the third demand: 'the reappropriation of the means of production . . . and free access to and control over knowledge, information, communications, and affects.'[19] This is, as Hardt and Negri acknowledge, the traditional socialist demand. It is indeed radical and it is that very radicalism which leaves it so out of step with the other two proposals. As such, it directly revives the fundamental questions Hardt and Negri raised but did not answer. What kind of movements could in fact develop the independent ideological and organizational capacities to reappropriate the means of production and communication from capital? What kind of movements could take state power and radically democratize it in the sense of transforming that power into a vehicle for mobilizing 'the multitudes' to democratize the economy and communications?

In spite of claims to the contrary, the 'Counter-Empire' of Hardt and Negri is about resistance to Empire, not its transformation. Resistance is of course welcome: it creates the space for hope and for the development of hope into a sustainable politics. But resistance as an end in itself carries a danger. It is not just that it does not go far enough, but that it risks exhausting what has been achieved. Moreover, to the extent that it encourages adventurism, it can detach militancy from its base rather than solidifying links with that base, with all the implications this has for isolation followed by repression. These are not abstract points. The inability to build on struggles, make them cumulative rather than sporadic, and limit the scope for state repression, has haunted the left since the student and worker struggles of the late 1960s and early 1970s. It is no less a concern today in contemplating the future of the anti-globalization movement.

The failure to move beyond resistance can, of course, hardly be placed at the doorstep of Hardt and Negri and the Negri-influenced autonomists; it is our collective failure. That Hardt and Negri seem to challenge that history and its politics is not the problem; the disappointment is that they do not go far enough.

There is a difference between acknowledging the failures of the past so we can move on, and elevating those details – as Hardt and Negri do in their discussion of the American working class – to victories. This not only avoids learning from historic defeats and blocks crucial questions, but contributes to raising barriers to finding a better strategy. Furthermore, one cannot help asking if the sentiment of treating resistance as strategy has itself affected the parameters of their theoretical investigation. There is something disturbingly pre-ordained about a major theorist of working-class autonomy like Negri, whose faith in the spontaneity of the working class was proven wrong before, rediscovering a fresh rationale for a similar politics today. The issue, we must emphasize, is not whether our commitment to human liberation drives our commitment to theoretical studies – this can be assumed. It is rather that we can only contribute to that commitment and vision if, as Marx insisted, our theory ruthlessly demands the truth of the world and we constantly revisit both our theory and practice as the *condition* of an ultimately effective praxis.

Hardt and Negri are true to this in their critiques of the false prophets of religious fundamentalism and academic postmodermism, which they see, despite the apparent polar opposition of those discourses, as paradoxically 'married' by virtue of having 'arisen not only at the same time, but also in response to the same situation', and by both being equally unable to recognize clearly the 'structures and logics of power in the contemporary world'. This is so because they approach this power in term of the binaries of 'hybridity versus purity, difference versus identity, mobility versus stasis'.[20] Hardt and Negri's own 'critical approach [which] addresses the need for a real ideological and material deconstruction of the imperial order'[21] is indeed much better. It is all the more unfortunate, therefore, that this book does not itself, for the reasons we have suggested, live up to the very standard its authors set for a critical approach, which, as they say, 'must seek continually to focus its powers on the nature of events and the real determinations of the imperial processes in motion today'.

Notes

1. Michael Hardt and Antonio Negri, *Empire*, Cambridge, MA: Harvard University Press 2000.
2. Ibid., p. xiv.
3. Ibid., pp. 9–10.
4. Ibid., p. 73.
5. Ibid., p. 83.
6. Ibid., p. 87.
7. Ibid., p. xvii.
8. Ibid., p. 205.
9. Ibid., p. xii.
10. Ibid., p. 285.
11. Ibid., p. 289.
12. Ibid., p. 293.
13. Ibid., pp. 268–9.
14. Robert Brenner, 'The Economics of Global Turbulence', *New Left Review* 1/229, pp. 1–264; Sam Gindin 'Turning Points and Starting Points: Brenner, Left Turbulence and Class Politics', *Working Classes/Global Realities: Social Register 2001*, ed. Colin Leys and Leo Panith, London: Merlin 2000.
15. *Empire*, pp. 362–3.
16. Ibid., p. 368.
17. Ibid., pp. 399–400.
18. Ibid., p. 400.
19. Ibid., pp. 406–7.
20. Ibid., pp. 149–50.
21. Ibid., pp. 47–8.

7

A Manifesto for Global Capital?

Ellen Meiksins Wood

A capitalist manifesto

Imagine a manifesto for global capital, written by a guru of globalization. Its object would be to present a picture of the world in which opposition to globalization and to capitalism itself would be futile, a world in which the best we can do is go with the flow, lie back and think of Nike.

What would be the essential propositions of such a manifesto? It would probably begin by insisting that the globalization of capital and the integration of the global economy have so transformed the world that the nation-state has become a fiction, as capital flows have far outreached the borders and the powers of the state. The world is now essentially ruled by the impersonal laws of the global market. To the extent that capital flows, and the movements of labour, still require some regulation, we may need such supranational institutions as the WTO and the IMF. But their role is to facilitate, not to dominate. To be sure, there are still a few flaws in the system, such as the disparity between rich and poor. But such problems will be solved not by resistance to global capital, not by less globalization, but, on the contrary, by more. Those who resist the relentless movement of capitalist globalization are doing much more harm than good.

We can come back in a moment to challenging this picture of the world. But let us first ask this: if the purpose of this analysis is to discourage opposition, at what point in the argument is resistance to global capital most effectively disabled? Of course, the general lesson we are supposed to draw from it is that capitalist globalization is an irresistible force and that opposition to what is practically a law of nature is futile and counterproductive. But an even more significant element in the argument is that it denies that there is any concentration of power in the global economy. Either power is an inappropriate category in defining the global-ized world, or power is so diffuse and immaterial that it might as well not exist at all. In either case, there is no target for opposition.

In this respect, the manifesto would be the equivalent on a global scale of much older 'pluralist' arguments in political science, challenged by Marxist theories of the state way back in the 1970s. According to that old liberal orthodoxy, there were no concentrations of class power in the liberal democratic state, only an infinite diffusion of countervailing powers throughout society. Now, we are told, even the state itself is effectively powerless, and political domination, no less than class rule, is a thing of the past. All political forces and organizational forms once designed to challenge the power of capital at the level of the state are even more irrelevant than they were in an earlier pluralist world, as irrevelant as the nation-state itself.

Such a manifesto would seem to imply that there is no effective possibility of opposition. The diffusion of power in capitalism has, to be sure, always presented a problem for oppositional forces. It has never been as easy to trace the class power of capital to a visible source as it was in precapitalist societies, where the capacity of economic exploitation rested on 'extra-economic' political and military powers. In capitalism, not only are the 'economic' and the 'political' separated, but the impersonal forces of 'the market' do much of capital's work. Nonetheless, as long as there was some identity between national states and national economies, struggles against capital could be directed not only against specific employ-ers 'at the point of production' but also against the capitalist class at a point of concentration in the state. It was, in fact, the essence of Marxist critiques of pluralist theories that the state did indeed constitute a point of concentration of capitalist power. But even if the state did once represent such a concentration of power and hence also a target of opposition, in today's globalized world, we are told, such possibilities of opposition no longer exist. What good are struggles at the point of production, when capital is organized in huge, transnational corporations? What good are political struggles when the nation-state is dead?

If it is really true that capitalist power is now a mystical force, immanent in the world and completely disembodied, everywhere and nowhere, it is the end of anti-capitalist struggle. Of course, the most sensible thing would be to embrace this ubiquitous force. But, in any case, resistance is futile. No amount of whistling in the dark about the insurrectional energies generated by globalization can change the fact that for us the game is over. The only opposition available to us is symbolic gesture and spectacle, or the internal refusal that gives a kind of spiritual freedom to the prisoner in chains. If there really is no material point at which the power of capital can be challenged, and with all forms of political action effectively disabled, the rule of capital is complete and eternal.

This counsel of surrender would be the message of a manifesto on behalf of global capital. It is also, like it or not, the message of Michael Hardt and Antonio Negri's *Empire*. This monumental and ambitious book has been read by supporters and critics alike as a relatively optimistic manifesto for oppositional forces in the globalized world. It has been praised as an eloquent voice for anti-capitalist movements. But for all its insistence on the possibilities of insurrection and the power of the 'multitude', it is much less persuasive as a call to opposition than as an argument for the futility of oppositional politics; and it has rather more to say about the irrelevance of old oppositional struggles and forces than about the possibilities of new ones.

'In this smooth space of Empire,' Hardt and Negri tell us, 'there is no *place* of power – it is both everywhere and nowhere. Empire is an *outopia* or really a *non-place*.'[1] What does this mean for the possibilities of opposition? We are told – in sweeping generalities – that, precisely because the power of Empire is everywhere and nowhere, 'the virtual center of Empire can be attacked from any point'.[2] What precisely this means remains unclear. But, as the argument proceeds, it is difficult to see what kind of opposition it allows, apart from spontaneous gestures on the part of an inchoate 'multitude', which, instead of resisting the processes of globalization, can somehow reorganize them toward new ends – though by what means and to what effect (apart from creating new 'subjectivities') remains a mystery.

We are told in rather more concrete terms what kinds of opposition are *not* possible. Political movements and organized working-class struggle are fruitless, especially local and national struggles (Hardt and Negri are very critical of anti-capitalist movements that focus on such struggles), because their traditional targets no longer exist. The simple fact is that, since there is no locus of power, there can be no real counter-power:

> The idea of counter-power and the idea of resistance against modern sovereignty in general thus becomes less and less possible. . . . A new type of resistance would have to be found that would be adequate to the dimensions of the new sovereignty. . . . Today, too, we can see that traditional forms of resistance, such as the institutional workers' organizations developed through the major part of the nineteenth and twentieth centuries have begun to lose their power.[3]

And so on. For all *Empire*'s lofty sentiments about new forms of contestation, this will be music to the ears of global capital. We are left with a mystical force opposed, if at all, by immaterial resistance.

But let us at least grant that *Empire* has its heart in the right place. Unlike our putative manifesto for global capital, it really does intend to celebrate, not to deny, the possibilities of contestation. The trouble is that its analysis of Empire denies us any such hope, no less effectively than the globalization manifesto does, and in alarmingly similar terms.

The problem begins with the very first premise on which the whole argument of *Empire* is based. 'Our basic hypothesis', write Hardt and Negri, 'is that sovereignty has taken a new form, composed of a series of national and supranational organisms united under a single logic of rule. This new global form of sovereignty is what we call Empire.'[4] Its primary symptom is '[t]he declining sovereignty of nation-states and their increasing inability to regulate economic and cultural exchanges'. This does not mean that sovereignty has disappeared together with the nation-state. It has simply changed its character. With the growth of transnational corporations, and global networks of production and circulation, 'which have undermined the powers of nation-states, state functions and constitutional elements have effectively been displaced to other levels and domains'.[5]

There is, of course, an important point here – which many

other commentators have also made – about the 'internationalization' of the state: that nation-states, like other institutions in the global system, are now responding not simply to the demands of national capital but to the 'logic' and requirement of global capital. Although we should not underestimate the persistence of national capital and, for that matter, the roots of transnational capital within it, this is certainly a point worth making. It does not require us to assume that the nation-state is effectively dying; and I have even heard Michael Hardt explain, in a public lecture, that globalization did not exclude the nation-state. The point, he insisted, was simply that the state was now subsumed in the logic of Empire.

That said, the essential argument of *Empire* is something else: at the very least, it requires us to accept that there is an inverse relation between the degree of globalization and the importance of the nation-state. And herein lies the problem, because surely the critical point about the 'internationalization' of the state is that the nation-state is useful to global capital not to the extent that it is *unable* to 'regulate economic and cultural exchanges'. On the contrary, it is useful precisely because it *can* intervene in the global economy and, indeed, remains the single most effective means of intervention. The essence of globalization is not the declining capacity but the unique *ability* of nation-states to organize the world for global capital. This reality, and global capital's inescapable need for territorial states to make possible its navigation of the world economy, is lost in the argument of *Empire*.

The book even seems indifferent to the coercive power concentrated in the state. That indifference is reflected in a conception of 'sovereignty' that allows Hardt and Negri to speak of the transfer of sovereign power away from the state, even though (a point on which *Empire* remains silent) it remains the dominant instrument of coercive force.

The first premise of *Empire*'s argument, then, is that the movements of sovereignty are parallel and conjoined with the movements of the economy, the networks of production and circulation. Give or take the odd time-lag or failure of synchronization, the two go hand-in-hand, so that the more global the economy becomes, the more global, too, will be the reach of sovereignty.

This account of the connection between the economic and

political moments of capitalism displays a fundamental misunderstanding of how the system works. The consequence of this
misunderstanding is that *Empire* never confronts the realities of
power or the possibilities of 'counter-power' in the world of global
capitalism. This, in fact, is the most striking characteristic of the
book: that, while purporting to be a study of power in the new
world of global capitalism, its argument depends on *evading* the
issue of power.

Economic hegemony and political sovereignty

Capitalism is distinctive among all social forms in its capacity
to extend its dominion beyond the limits of political authority,
by purely 'economic' means. Capital's drive for relentless self-
expansion depends on this unique capacity, which is expressed in
both capitalist class domination and in capitalist imperialism. At
the level of class relations, capital can exercise its power over
labour without the direct application of coercive force. Unlike
class domination in non-capitalist forms, where the capacity to
extract surplus labour depended on direct 'extra-economic' coercion, capitalism can rely on the economic coercions imposed by
the market dependence of direct producers and particularly
propertyless workers, who must sell their labour for a wage simply
to gain access to the means of their own subsistence. Much
the same applies to the new forms of imperialism created by
capitalism, which no longer require direct colonial rule but can
generally rely on the manipulation of economic forces.

   The distinctive mode of economic domination made possible
by capitalism – which, indeed, constitutes capitalism – has produced, and depended upon, a complex relationship between
economic force and political sovereignty. Capitalism's purely
'economic' mode of exploitation, the growing commodification
of life, the regulation of social relations by the impersonal 'laws'
of the market, have meant the emergence of a distinct 'economic'
sphere, formally separate from the 'political'. This has also created a formally distinct political sphere and a state with a more
clearly defined territorial sovereignty than was possible in non-
capitalist societies. At the same time, many social functions that
once fell within the scope of state administration or communal
regulation have now been left to the 'economy'. This applies most

particularly, of course, to the organization of production and distribution. But, as social life is increasingly commodified and regulated by the 'laws' of the 'economy', its requirements shape every aspect of life and the organization of time itself.

On the face of it, then, the emergence of an 'economy', while it also creates a separate 'political' sphere, seems at the same time to impoverish that sphere, to remove much of human life from its orbit and, therefore, also to put most aspects of everyday life outside the range of democratic accountability. The disconnection between the economy and sovereignty has also permitted the economic reach of capital to far exceed its political grasp and to extend far beyond the geographic boundaries of territorial sovereignty.

Yet here we encounter a paradox. Capitalist appropriation still requires the support of extra-economic coercion, and a state operating at arms length is still required to supply the ultimate coercive force that capital needs but lacks. Capitalism is a uniquely anarchic system, and capital is unique among dominant classes in the degree to which it lacks direct coercive power. Yet capitalism, more than any other social form, needs regularity and predictability in its daily transactions, which can be guaranteed only by a closely regulated legal and political order. Capitalism also depends on extra-economic practices and institutions to compensate for its own disruptive tendencies, for the social ravages of the market, and for the propertylessness of the majority on which capitalist power depends.

The trouble is that no form of sovereignty has yet been devised that can fill these needs apart from the territorial state, which functions on behalf of global capital no less than for local and national capital. The disconnection between the economic and political moments of capital not only makes it possible for capital to extend its economic reach but also requires it to rely on local states to serve its political needs.

This complex relation is not reducible to any simple formula. But the least helpful of all is the easy assumption that, as capital expands its reach, it pushes out the boundaries of sovereignty. It would, again, be far more accurate to say that, on the one hand, the expansion of capital is possible precisely because it can detach itself from sovereignty in a way that no other social form can; and, on the other hand, the same detachment makes it both possible and necessary for capital's economic hegemony to be supported by territorial states. That, we might say, is one of capitalism's many contradictions.

Capitalism emerged as the 'political' and 'economic' separated, and it continues to rely on that separation, which makes possible the unbounded expansion of capitalist appropriation by purely economic means. While the national organization of capitalist economies has remained stubbornly persistent, this has not precluded the wide-ranging expansion of capitalist appropriation far beyond national borders. At the same time, the nation-state has remained an indispensable instrument – perhaps the *only* indispensable 'extra-economic' instrument – of global capital.

At the level of the national economy and nation-state, the complex relation between capitalist appropriation and the extra-economic force it requires to sustain it is relatively straightforward, if fraught with contradictions. There is a more or less clear division of labour: capital appropriates, while the 'neutral' state enforces the system of property, and propertylessness, on which capital's purely economic power of appropriation depends. But the connections become more complicated as capital extends its geographic reach while still depending on more local and territorially limited powers of administration and enforcement. We are just now beginning to learn about the complexities and contradictions of that relationship beyond the borders of the nation-state and in the new system of capitalist imperialism.[6]

The first, and what should be the most immediately obvious, point about the new imperialism is that it does *not* involve the disappearance or even the decline of the nation-state. On the contrary, this new imperialism, in contrast to older forms of colonial empire, depends more than ever on a system of multiple and formally sovereign national states. The very fact that 'globalization' has extended capital's purely economic powers far beyond the range of any single nation-state means that global capital requires *many* nation-states to perform the necessary administrative and coercive functions.

Global capital benefits from globalization but it does not organize globalization. Capitalist enterprises have difficulty managing their own international operations, let alone the whole global economy. There would be no *global* economy at all without a system of states to administer and enforce it and to enable global capital to navigate the global market. To suggest that these functions have moved to other 'levels and domains' is to deny the realities of power. Even a moment's reflection shows that no transnational organization has come close to assuming the indispensable functions of the nation-state in maintaining social order, least of all the function of coercion that underlies all others. No conceivable form of 'global governance' could provide the kind of daily order or the conditions of accumulation that capital needs. The world today, in fact, is more than ever a world of nation-states. The political form of globalization (of Empire?) is not a global state or global sovereignty but a global system of multiple states and local sovereignties, structured in a complex relation of domination and subordination.

Empire or imperialism, peace or war?

Today, of course, the imperial hegemon is the US, and *Empire*'s treatment of US democracy and US imperialism is the most striking testimony to its misconceptions about the nature of capitalist domination. It is here, too, that we see most vividly something like the old 'pluralist' theory of politics transformed into a theory of global Empire. 'Empire', we are told, 'can only be conceived as a universal republic, a network of powers and counterpowers structured in a boundless and inclusive architecture'. And just as the liberal democratic state in pluralist theory had nothing to do with class domination, in Hardt and Negri's global pluralism 'This imperial expansion has nothing to do with imperialism, nor with those state organisms designed for conquest, pillage, genocide, colonization, and slavery.'[7] No doubt the 'expansive moments of Empire have been bathed in tears and blood', but Empire is still fundamentally different from imperialism. It is, at least in tendency, the principles of a 'democratic republic' expanding outward to embrace the whole world, with all its egalitarian and inclusive impulses. The basis, in principle if not in practice, of this new mode of imperial expansion, 'the expansive tendency of the democratic republic', is the 'idea of peace'.

Let us postpone for a moment a consideration of *Empire*'s conception of democracy and the 'democratic republic', which is the source of a new form of Empire. Consider, first, the 'idea of

peace' in today's imperial order. Hardt and Negri are certainly
right to say that the current US Empire is something very different
from older forms of colonial imperialism. But it is different in just
the way that capitalist domination differs from earlier forms.
Direct colonial rule is certainly not the form of this new imperialism. Just as the class relation between capital and labour is not a
relation of legal or political domination and subordination, such
as the relation between feudal lord and peasant, the new imperialism is not an 'extra-economic' relation between rulers and
subjects, conquerors and conquered. It does not typically impose
its sovereignty directly on subject peoples or territories. Instead,
it operates by manipulating the economic forces of 'the market'
to the advantage of imperial capital.

But here we come to our paradox again. The global system of
economic coercion, while it can reach far beyond political sovereignty, cannot function without the help of an 'extra-economic'
apparatus of administration and coercion. Yet no such apparatus
exists that can encompass the whole global economy, nor is such
an apparatus even conceivable in the foreseeable future. So the
new imperialism relies on the powers of administration and
enforcement embodied in many legally sovereign states, both
imperial and subordinate powers.

This arrangement poses problems of its own. If multiple states
will guard the world economy, who will guard the guardians?
Market forces manipulated by the dominant powers can certainly
go a long way toward keeping subordinate regimes in line. But,
not only are local states susceptible to their own internal pressures
and oppositional forces, even 'the market' itself must be kept
firmly in place by coercion. The ultimate guarantee is the military
force of the one remaining superpower. But, since, by definition,
this is a global empire in which no single power of coercion can
be everywhere at once and all the time, the new imperialism has
required new military doctrines too.

The first premise of the current US military doctrine, with
roots that go back to the end of World War Two, is that the US
must have such massive military superiority that no other power,
friend or foe, will seek to challenge or equal it as a global or
regional hegemon. The object is not simply to deter attack but to
discourage any rivalry. This degree of military supremacy requires
new strategies. The US has consequently been experimenting

with the use of military force designed not simply to capture or control territory, nor to extend the sovereignty of its state, but rather to shape the political environment throughout the global system of multiple states. It does this not only directly, by forcing the restructuring of the regimes that are its targets, but also indirectly – not least, by forging coalitions or alliances in which it remains the dominant power – to organize relations among states, as well as political alignments within them.

But beyond any such specific aims, the new imperialist strategy seeks to contain the global system of multiple states by regularly displaying its massive military force, to show that, if it cannot be everywhere all the time, it can go anywhere, any time, and cause massive damage. The result has been a pattern of military interventions in which means are disconnected from any particular ends, a pattern of wars without objectives, exit strategies or geographical boundaries.

The 'war against terrorism' is the model US war in the era of the new imperialism. (Perhaps the most striking comment on the thesis of *Empire* is that, in the lecture to which I alluded earlier, the central theme of which was war, Hardt made no mention at all of the US campaign in Afghanistan, then still in progress. The thesis of *Empire* obliged Hardt to treat all modern wars as internal to 'Empire' and hence essentially as civil wars. Is it possible that the Hardt/Negri thesis simply cannot accommodate the military actions of an imperial nation-state, and least of all the 'democratic' USA?) It is not some flight of poetic fancy that has led hawks in the White House, at least privately, to call this campaign 'Operation Infinite War'. It is clearly meant to be a war with no constraints of time or geography, with, according to Donald Rumsfeld, at least fifty states as its potential targets and likely to last beyond our lifetimes. That vision has been given official status in a new Bush Doctrine, outlined unambiguously in the administration's *National Security Strategy*, issued in September 2002. The new imperial hegemony, commanding a global economy administered by multiple states, requires war without end – in purpose or time.

There is nothing benign or democratic about this mode of imperialist war, nor is it an accidental and sporadic feature of the new imperialism. It is, in fact, an essential requirement, the direct antithesis of the 'idea of peace'. The new imperial form, which is rooted in US democracy, may not (or not always) require wars of outright military conquest, but it does require a kind of Hobbesian state of war, not necessarily endless fighting but an endless *possibility* of war. The nature of war, as Hobbes puts it, does not necessarily consist in 'actual fighting' but in 'the known disposition thereto, during all the time there is no assurance to the contrary'.[8] The open-ended threat of war, its possibility anywhere at any time, is as close as the new imperialism can come to coercive enforcement of order in a world of multiple states. This 'state of war' has, if anything, become more rather than less important to US hegemony, as challenges on other fronts – economic, political, cultural, ecological – especially from regional blocs like the European Union, to say nothing of aspiring rivals like China, force it back onto its one indisputable superiority, its overwhelming military power.

Democracy and the power of the 'multitude'

Empire's conception of Empire is inextricably bound up with its understanding of democracy. Here, too, the problem is a failure to confront the nature of capitalist power and how it reconfigures the political world.

The failure to see the concentrations of power embodied in the state is mirrored in the way *Empire* conceives the power of the formless and disorganized 'multitude'. In effect, the counter-power of the multitude, like the power of Empire, is everywhere and nowhere. As capitalism comes to fruition in the realization of the world market, say Hardt and Negri, and finds its proper political form in the decline of the nation state, as we move 'from imperialism to Empire, and from the nation-state to the political regulation of the global market', there is a historic shift in the possibilities of struggle.[9]

'Having achieved the global level,' we are told, 'capitalist development is faced directly with the multitude, without mediation.' Without the barrier of the state, 'the situation of struggle is completely open'.

If this is meant to be something more than a philosophical abstraction, if it is meant to be an observation about the realities, or even the tendencies, of power in the world today, it is hard to think of anything more vacuous. However global the market has become, there is no evidence that sovereignty has moved with it in parallel, or that capital needs the state less than it once did, or that the state is mediating any less forcefully in the relations between capital and labour than it ever did before. Anti-capitalist protestors in Genoa (to cite just one example) will not have failed to notice some fairly potent mediations by the state.

We can accept that Hardt and Negri's formulation is intended as an optimistic statement about the possibility of transforming capitalist globalization into a truly democratic world order. But to underestimate, and even deny, the mediations of the state as a reality facing oppositional struggles is surely no basis for optimism. In this account, the multitude's power seems to lie in its powerlessness, while any real possibility of oppositional power, a real counter-power in the real world, is effectively denied.

In fact, as *Empire*'s argument proceeds, it is difficult to avoid the suspicion that the power of the 'multitude' is indeed just a philosophical abstraction, and that this power is *nowhere* rather more than it is everywhere. This impression becomes very strong when Hardt and Negri talk about democracy and the 'idea of an Empire that is also a democratic republic',[10] a curious notion that depends on misconceptions about the democratic republic no less than about empire. Particularly in their understanding of the US Constitution, which for them embodies the essence of the modern democratic republic and the Empire that emanates from it, the concept of democracy is dangerously diluted. Democratic power is here no less inchoate and mystical than the power of Empire.

Hardt and Negri attribute to the US the birth of a new form of sovereignty, an 'immanent' power as against the 'transcendant' sovereignty of modern Europe. This power, they explain, emanates from the 'productive synergies' of the multitude – that is, it is a power *made* by the multitude rather than imposed upon it. Of course, the realization and exercise of such power, especially given the 'conflictive and plural nature of the multitude itself', requires the imposition of controls, which constantly threaten the multitude's sovereignty.[11] But this contradiction is countered by an 'expansive tendency' which, in contrast to other forms of expansion, is open and inclusive. 'In other words, when it expands, this new sovereignty does not annex or destroy the other powers it encounters but on the contrary opens itself to them,

including them in the network', constantly reforming the network
of powers and the basis of consensus.[12]

This expansive tendency of the democratic republic created by
the US Constitution, they argue, is 'the hinge that links the
principle of a democratic republic to the idea of Empire. It
creates, in principle, the possibility of an open and inclusive
'Empire', different in its modalities and consequences from older
forms of imperial conquest and oppression, a principle of Empire
that expresses the sovereignty of the multitude.[13] So US democracy is the first form of sovereignty explicitly rooted in the power
of the multitude, and its way of dealing with the powers that
thwart it is not to impose itself on them from without but rather
to include them in its always open embrace.

The problem with this analysis is not that it is wrong about the
novelty and originality of US democracy. Nor do Hardt and Negri
entirely neglect the rather less benign ways in which that democracy, with its own brand of imperial expansiveness, has actually
comported itself in the world – though they have remarkably little
to say about those bloody 'moments' of expansion. The trouble
lies rather in a misidentification of this democracy's novelty, and
what it tells us about the configuration of power in the modern
capitalist world, or the possibilities of democratic struggles against
it.

The novelty of US democracy does not, in the first place, lie in
the notion that sovereign power derives from the people, or the
'multitude' that constitutes itself as the 'people' in its founding
political act. This was not in itself a novel idea in Western political
traditions before the US Constitution. If anything, it was a commonplace – but one so flexible that it could underwrite everything
from popular democracy to absolute monarchy. True, it could,
among other things, justify the right of revolution against tryanny,
though typically without establishing democracy instead. But even
an umbiguously absolutist argument like that of Thomas Hobbes
had as its premise the notion that sovereign power is constituted
by the multitude. Here, that notion is used not to defend the
power of the people but, on the contrary, to insist on their
obligation to submit unconditionally to the sovereign power they
have supposedly created. In Hobbes's argument, the unconditional alienation of power that establishes sovereignty is the only
political act of which the multitude is capable.

To be sure, there is in principle a very great difference between a conception of sovereignty constituted by a transfer of powers unconditionally from the multitude to an absolute monarch, and, by contrast, a conception of popular sovereignty as inalienable. There is a big difference between the notion that democracy is the only legitimate form of government, because power belongs by nature to the people, and, by contrast, the idea that any *de facto* power is legitimate, because as long as it exists, it must be understood as having been constituted by the people, who are therefore obligated to obey. The latter is, more or less, Hobbes's view.

But the critical point here is that democracy does not inevitably follow from the notion that sovereignty is constituted by the multitude. This idea is no less compatible with profoundly undemocratic forms of government. In *Empire*'s conception of democracy there is a slippage, an apparent disregard for everything that stands between the multitude and democracy, everything that the Western state, not just Western political thinkers, has interposed between them. In the end, the conception of popular sovereignty outlined by Hardt and Negri turns out to be hardly less notional and immaterial than the 'popular sovereignty' that underlay some earlier conceptions of absolutist monarchy.

The use that Hardt and Negri make of Spinoza, apparently *Empire*'s primary philosophical inspiration, already suggests a certain indifference to the difficulties inherent in the flexible concept of sovereignty constituted by the multitude. While Hobbes, they argue, 'plays a foundational role in the modern construction of a transcendent political apparatus',[14] Spinoza is the philosopher of 'immanence', the philosopher who best expresses the idea that all power and authority are inherent in, and emanate from, the multitude. Yet both philosophers started from the same premise: that, as Spinoza puts it in the *Tractatus Theologico-Politicus*, 'each has as much right as he has power' (ll.8). Hobbes himself is reported to have commented ruefully, on reading the *Tractatus* when it first came out in 1670, that Spinoza had outdone him, having 'cut through him a barre's length, for he [Hobbes] durts not write so boldly.'[15] And it is hard to deny that Spinoza was even bolder, or more direct, than Hobbes on this point. The principle that might makes right can certainly be used to justify republican government no less (and no more) than tyrannical monarchy. It simply means that whoever has power has the right to power, just as anyone who loses power has, by definition, lost it legitimately. But this applies no less to Hobbes's argument than to Spinoza's, however much the former preferred monarchy and the latter republican government.

Throughout its history, the notion of sovereignty constituted by the multitude has been notoriously flexible; and, by itself, it does not get us very far. The mobilization of this idea in *Empire* leaves it no less vague and open-ended than it ever was and tells us very little about how, in practice or even in theory, to translate that notional sovereignty into a substantive global democracy. But even short of that, Hardt and Negri's discussion of popular sovereignty disguises what is truly distinctive about US democracy.

The US redefinition of democracy

The notion of popular sovereignty today may no longer be compatible with absolute monarchy, but the idea of democracy is certainly compatible with class rule by the rich. This is the very opposite of what it signified in its original meaning, and the foundation of the United States is largely responsible for that redefinition. The US notion of democracy was the first to unite formal rule 'by the people' with substantive class rule, the first to incorporate the peculiar separation of the economic and political that capitalism alone makes possible. Hardt and Negri's tendency to romanticize US democracy rests on the same misapprehensions about the nature of capitalist power as does their conception of Empire.

Much of Western political thought has, from the beginning, concerned itself with limiting democracy. The need to limit popular power by means of oligarchic principles was already a central concern of ancient Greek and Roman political thought, and especially in the concept of the 'mixed constitution', of which Hardt and Negri are so fond. In the early modern era and thereafter, Western political theorists sought new ways of grappling with the problem of limiting democracy, balancing the notion that power originates in the people with varying degrees of limits on popular power, up to and including its complete and unconditional surrender. The US Constitution represents a major milestone in that history – not just the history of democracy but of limits on popular power. It is not surprising that the ideal model for US 'democracy' was not the ancient democracy of Athens but the 'mixed constitution' of republican Rome, which never claimed to be a democracy. The emblematic formula, The Senate and the Roman People (SPQR), nicely summed up the basic principle of this 'mixed constitution': the subjection of plebeian citizens to oligarchic rule.

The idea of democracy forged in the American Revolution did indeed transform the idea of popular sovereignty and the notion that the free individuals who constitute the 'multitude' are the basic constituents of sovereign power. But it did so in a far more ambiguous way than Hardt and Negri allow. Even if we leave aside the exclusion of slaves and women from the political community, the new form of democracy had as much to do with disempowering the multitude as with acknowledging its sovereignty.

In a revolutionary situation, with a multitude accustomed to political activism and even democratic local institutions before the Revolution, popular sovereignty threatened to become not just power exercised in the last instance and *in extremis* but a principle of everyday politics. In these circumstances, even the most undemocratic of the 'Founding Fathers' no longer had the option of advocating the complete and unconditional alienation of power by the multitude to an elite. But they did find a way of redefining democracy so that it was compatible with the alienation of power. Until this reformulation, any alienation of power by the multitude, however conditional, was by definition something other than democracy. Democratic critics of the Federalists regarded the constitutional formula, 'we, the people', as an assault on democracy and not an expression of it, because they understood it to mean that the sovereignty of the multitude would effectively be transferred from the people to a distant central state.

In general, the Founding Fathers did not want or claim to be founding a democracy. But when the exigencies of debate with more democratic elements forced a rhetorical shift, they simply redefined democracy. Their discourse oscillated between denouncing democracy, and (less often) calling the new republic a 'representative democracy', an idea that, to the ancient Greeks who invented democracy, would have been a contradiction in terms. In the process of this rhetorical shift, the Federalists created a novel idea of democracy, which allowed for, and even required, the alienation of power.

The Federalists did not simply argue (as, for instance, Tom Paine did) that representation is a necessary expedient in a large and complex society; or even that the right to cultivate one's own garden, while others take on public responsibilities, is a necessary condition of freedom. The object of representative democracy was, quite explicitly, to distance the sovereign multitude as much as possible from the real exercise of power, which would remain in the hands of an elite.

The central issue here was not the formal difference between direct and representative democracy. The essential question was how to preserve elite rule in the context of 'popular sovereignty'. Even the more democratic James Madison, in his classic *Federalist* no. 10, argues not that representation is needed in a large republic but that a large republic is preferable because it requires representation. In fact, the larger the better, because that allows for a smaller ratio of representatives to represented, so that the 'better sort of men' (and, of course, it is only men) will govern. Alexander Hamilton makes the underlying class assumptions more explicit, by arguing against any system of 'actual' representation and insisting, for example, that merchants are the 'natural' representatives of craftsmen and labourers.

'Democracy' in this new meaning was, then, already at one remove from the classic conception of 'rule by the people'. But even more significant was the redefinition of 'the people' itself. Just as the *kratos* or power in 'democracy' had taken on a different meaning, so too did the *demos*. In the ancient conception of democracy, the *demos* was not only a political category – a body of citizens endowed with certain civic rights and powers – but a *social* category: the common people or even the poor. So 'democracy' was, in effect, a form of class rule, in which the poor ruled the rich, and this is certainly how its anti-democratic critics perceived it. This was the sense in which democracy continued to be understood well into the modern era, and why 'democracy' was generally a dirty word among elites.

The American experience began to change all that. The *demos* or 'people' was increasingly evacuated of its social meaning. (Hardt and Negri's notion of the 'multitude', in place of, say, the working class, has much in common with this desocialized conception of the 'people'.) In the new meaning it was even possible, as Hamilton had demonstrated, to identify democracy with rule by the rich. Eventually, even an attenuated 'power of, or rule by, the people' ceased to be the main criterion of democracy, as the emphasis shifted away from the active exercise of popular power to the passive enjoyment of constitutional rights and procedural safeguards. From then on, even rabid anti-democrats in the traditional meaning could happily claim to be democrats in the American sense.

Today, the right to vote itself seems to have little bearing on the essence of 'democracy', as barely half the US electorate considers it worthwhile to make the effort even once in four years. With the current 'war on terrorism' the US seems bent on teaching the world (not for the first time) that even civil liberties are not an essential requirement of democracy. In the end, all that counts is the hegemony of capital and the 'free market'. In the Bush regime, we have the most transparent identification of 'democracy' with the rule of capital, and the interests of oil in particular. Even Alexander Hamilton would balk at this, and the US has certainly come a long way from the 'representative democracy' established by the founders. But recent developments in the story of democracy have clearly discernible roots in the original redefinition.

Democracy and the Empire of capital

Yet the redefinition of democracy pioneered in the US was not simply a clever play on words. No amount of verbal trickery alone would have made it possible to conceive of 'democracy' in this new way. No earlier society could have solved the age-old problem of political relations between 'mass' and 'elite' as the Americans did. A 'formal' democracy devoid of social meaning was not even conceptually possible in ancient Greece or medieval Europe, where class relations were directly determined by 'extra-economic' powers.

A peasant-citizen, such as existed in Athenian democracy, was, by virtue of his citizenship, spared the principal forms of extra-economic class exploitation that have burdened peasantries throughout history. So democracy did have an essential bearing on class relations. Conversely, a medieval European peasant with full political rights would not, by definition, have been a serf, nor could there have been a feudal lordship had peasants enjoyed full civic rights. A democratic feudalism would have been a contradiction in terms. Only capitalism, with its distinctive relation between political and economic 'spheres', has permitted this new concept of democracy, in which democratic rights are confined to a 'formal' political sphere, while class exploitation remains intact in other domains.

But while capitalism allows 'democracy' to be confined within a limited sphere of operation, the division of labour between the power of appropriation and the power of coercion that makes this possible also makes the state a vital organ for the capitalist class. Capitalist exploitation can certainly go on in the economic sphere without interference, even where all citizens are juridically equal and even in conditions of universal suffrage. But capitalism relies on the state to create the conditions of accumulation and enforcement that capital cannot create for itself. However much class domination has shifted to the 'economy', capital would be very uneasy if extra-economic coercive powers were in the hands of a truly democratic state, a state dominated by the *demos* not merely as a civic category but as a social one.

The US represents the model capitalist democracy. It combines, in ideological conception and in practical reality, the formal sovereignty of the 'multitude' with the substantive rule of capital. If this democracy is characterized by an 'expansive tendency', which finds expression in a new kind of Empire, that tendency belongs not to the sovereign multitude but to the rule of capital. Up to now, US democracy has served capital well by preserving the balance between 'formal' democracy and capitalist class rule, both outside and inside the state. But the new world order suggests that this balance is potentially in danger.

The old relation between political and economic power which made it possible for capitalism to tolerate formal democracy has now been disrupted. The division of labour between the state and capital has been disturbed. On the one hand, the separation of political and economic power, which has allowed capital to extend its reach around the globe and across political boundaries, has also produced a growing gap between the economic powers of capital and the political powers required to sustain them. On the other hand, the consequence of a globalized economy has been that states have become more, not less, involved in the management of economic circuits, and that capital has become more, not less, dependent on organization of the economy by a system of many local states.

To manage the global economy, capital needs local states not only in the imperial centre but throughout the global system. Local democratic shifts such as the recent elections in Latin America, and especially in Brazil, can upset the imperial balance. It may seem paradoxical to say so, but even the US reliance on massive military force to send the world a message about its hegemony testifies that something is wrong in the balance between the imperial power of capital and its political sovereignty. Military force like this is a very blunt instrument and completely unsuited to supply the daily legal and political conditions for capital accumulation.

In this new world order, democracy, even in its limited form, is likely to be under growing attack. There has already been an assault on liberal democracy, an attack on civil liberties in the US and elsewhere. In a state of perpetual war, even the formal democracy of capitalist societies is under threat – in the so-called war against terrorism as it was in the Cold War.

But this also means that local and national struggles are more important now than ever before. This is so not in spite but because of globalization, because global capital depends not on some mystical power which is everywhere and nowhere but on very concrete concentrations of power. In the gap between economic circuits and political sovereignty, there are new possibilities for oppositional struggle. Global capital's dependence on local states may be its greatest vulnerability; and nothing could be more threatening to capitalist power than struggles, both inside and outside the state, for a truly democratic sovereignty, a genuinely popular sovereignty that transforms the balance of class power in the state, in imperial powers as well as subordinate ones.

This, of course, requires something more than symbolic gestures by a mystical 'multitude'. Current anti-capitalist movements can do much to change the political climate; and it is, of course, vital to confront global capital at every available point – economic, political, cultural and ideological. But truly effective oppositional struggle must recognize that the power of capital is not just everywhere and nowhere, and that it still requires its point of concentration in the state. This also means that, while old forms of working-class and socialist organization cannot proceed as before, any effective 'counter-power' will still need political organization and a solid social base.

Fighting power with counter-power may seem harder to accomplish than the formless opposition Hardt and Negri have in mind, but it also promises to have more concrete results. An analysis of power as it operates in the real world of global capitalism is certainly sobering. But it also carries a more optimistic message about the possibilities of opposition, because, unlike *Empire*, it allows us both the targets and the means of struggle.

Notes

1. Michael Hardt and Antonio Negri, *Empire*, Cambridge, MA: Harvard University Press 2000, p. 190.
2. Ibid., p. 59.
3. Ibid., p. 308.
4. Ibid., p. xii.
5. Ibid., p. 307.
6. This argument and the discussion of the new imperialism that follows is based on my book, *Empire of Capital*, London: Verso 2003.
7. *Empire*, pp. 166–7.
8. Thomas Hobbes, *Leviathan*, Cambridge: Cambridge University Press, p. 88.
9. *Empire*, p. 237.
10. Ibid., p. 167.
11. Ibid., p. 165.
12. Ibid., p. 166.
13. Ibid., pp. 164–6.
14. Ibid., p. 83.
15. John Aubrey, 'The Life of Thomas Hobbes of Malmesbury', in John Buchanan-Brown, ed., Aubrey's *Brief Lives*.

You Can't Build a New Society with a Stanley Knife

Malcolm Bull

Recently released on parole from Rebibbia prison in Rome, Antonio Negri has unimpeachable revolutionary credentials. In the 1970s, he was the leading theorist of Potere Operaio and later of the Autonomia movement. But in 1979, the kidnapping and execution of the Christian Democratic leader Aldo Moro by the Red Brigades gave the Italian authorities the pretext for the indiscriminate repression of the extra-parliamentary left. Thousands of activists were arrested on political charges; Negri was sentenced to prison, only to be released under parliamentary immunity when elected as a Radical MP. Escaping to France, where he had the support of Deleuze and Guattari, he continued his academic career in Paris (Michael Hardt was a student) until 1997 when he voluntarily returned to Italy to serve out the remainder of his sentence.

Negri's attempt to re-theorize the autonomist strategy began during his first spell in prison with a study of Spinoza. He found in Spinoza a distinction (lost in English translations) between *potentia* (strength, force, creative activity) and *potestas* (authority, command, sovereignty). According to Spinoza, God's power (*potentia*) is his essence, and what we conceive to be in his power (*potestas*) necessarily exists. For Negri this does not just mean that since God is necessarily creative his creation is necessary too; it involves the subordination of *potestas* to the continuing actualization of *potentia*: God's sovereignty over the world is, in reality, nothing other than his world-making. The political import of this distinction emerges in Spinoza's unfinished *Political Treatise*, where, Negri claims, the multitude becomes 'a productive essence' and the *potestas* of the sovereign is the *potentia* of the people.[1]

Here, the old autonomist strategy of disengagement from existing structures of authority found a new justification. The proletariat may have given way to Spinoza's multitude, and the language of economics to that of jurisprudence, but the basic point was unchanged: taking power and making power are the same thing. The revoluntionary potential of this idea was affirmed in *Insurgencies* where Negri pointed out that the English and American revolutions had been inspired by just such a doctrine – the republican theory of liberty, with its emphasis on the constituent power of the citizenry. In the brief passage 'from resistance to revolution, from associationism to the constitution of political bodies . . . from *militiae* to the armies', was the proof that *potentia* could become *potestas* overnight.[2] All that Marx had needed to add to what J. G. A. Pocock called the 'Atlantic republican tradition' was the idea that the political always includes the social. Now, 'political space becomes social space', and with creative free labour as its subject, constituent power is 'the revolution itself'.[3]

In *Empire*, this argument is applied to globalization. The new world order represents a new form of imperial sovereignty akin to the mixed constitution of the United States and 'composed of a series of national and supranational organisms united under a single logic of rule'.[4] The account of the way in which these 'organisms' – the United States itself, the G8, the UN, the NGOS, the multinationals and the media conglomerates – exercise their authority is left rather vague, but in a sense it does not matter. Empire, like other forms of sovereignty (*imperium* in Spinoza), is only the power of the people writ large. In globalization, alternatives to capitalism are not defeated so much as given new opportunity to work on a global scale: 'The creative forces of the multitude that sustain Empire are also capable of autonomously constructing a counter-Empire, an alternative political organization of global flows and exchange'.[5]

It is easy to see why *Empire* has proved the most successful work of political theory to come from the left for a generation. Not only is it written with unusual energy, clarity, and wit, but it addresses directly the central political issue of the moment – the perceived distance between ordinary people trying to live in the way they want to, and the systems of power that defeat them. By simultaneously redefining globalization as a form of sovereignty and recasting the autonomist project in the republican tradition, Hardt and Negri offer an exceptionally optimistic analysis of the problem: remote as it may seem, sovereignty is nothing that a few like-minded people cannot create for themselves. Today's anti-capitalist protests may look like mob violence, but that is half the point: the street mobs made America too; this is counter-Empire in the making.

Nevertheless, the structure of counter-Empire remains obscure. Hardt and Negri distance themselves from those who merely want to 'defend the local and construct barriers to capital'.[6] But although their reinterpretation of autonomy involves more than freedom from the constraints of the market, it is still recognizably part of the late twentieth-century reworking of liberalism. Negri's rediscovery of republican thought in the early 1980s paralleled that of Quentin Skinner in Britain, and the retrieval of antifederalism by libertarians in the United States. In no case did this involve the repudiation of the idea of negative liberty, just a renewed emphasis on the point that people can be free only if they also have an ongoing capacity for self-government. For Skinner this meant a call to active citizenship, while for Negri it involved the reaffirmation of the antifederalist view that the constituent power of the citizen is not irretrievably transferred to the sovereign through some contract or constitution. The constituent power of the multitude is inalienable, it remains, as Negri writes in *Insurgencies*, 'an irresistible provocation to imbalance, restlessness, and historical ruptures'.[7]

But this is not the Marxist revolution to which Negri was once committed. Although hailed by Slavoj Žižek as 'the *Communist Manifesto* for our time', *Empire* is more Jeffersonian than Marxist. Like those who invoke the *Declaration of Independence* against the federal government, Hardt and Negri focus on the contradictions generated by liberalism's global sovereignty: the nuclear bomb (a standing affront to militias as well as to pacifists), the continuing existence of immigration controls, the reliance of global business and media interests on government support and regulation. Cheerfully appropriating the slogans of national neo-liberalism

for use against global neo-liberalism, Hardt and Negri proclaim:
'Now that the most radical conservative opponents of big government have collapsed under the weight of the paradox of their
position, we want to pick up their banners. . . . It is our turn now
to cry "Big government is over!" '[8]

With its repeated affirmation that we do not have to accept the
world as we find it, and that we can remake it to suit ourselves,
Empire is certainly inspirational reading. But what, if anything, it
might inspire someone to do is hard to say. Because Hardt and
Negri's version of republican liberty is a theory of power rather
than of rights it does not easily translate into talk of duties.
(Unlike Skinner, they cannot call for laws forcing us to exercise
our rights.) Furthermore, their analysis of power is not one that
lends itself to judgements about the way it should be exercised.
Both of these problems are inherited from Spinoza, whose theological metaphysics dictated that, since all power is God's power,
power must be co-extensive with natural right. In a state of nature
everyone therefore has as much right as they have the power to
exercise, limited only by the antagonist power of others. The
formation of the commonwealth involves no transfer of natural
right to the sovereign (as in social contract theory) merely an
aggregation of power, and thus of right, that increases the power
of the commonwealth over nature and over the individuals within
it. Civil right is natural right and natural right is power. As Negri
puts it in *Insurgencies*: 'the law precedes the constitution, the
people's autonomy lives before its formalization. It is the Tartar
who founds freedom, in the experience of his own right.'[9]

The belief that civil right is unalienated power is fundamental
to Negri's entire rethinking of the autonomist programme. But as
many commentators have pointed out, Spinoza's theory licenses
tyranny as much as democracy, counter-revolution as well as revolution. Whoever exercises sovereignty has the right to do so for as
long as they have the power to maintain it. By replacing Marx with
Spinoza, Negri preserves the revolutionary creed at the expense
of its justification. For Spinoza, there is no point at which either
the individual or the multitude is alienated from something that
is naturally or rightfully theirs, so no one has any claim to power
that they do not happen to possess. If someone develops larger
muscles, buys a bigger gun, or stages a successful revolution, power
and right are redistributed accordingly. That is all there is to it.

Spinoza, it is no surprise to discover, was Henry Kissinger's preferred political philosopher. Whether he was Mrs Thatcher's favourite as well, I do not know, but on Negri's reading he ought to have been. For someone who claimed that 'there is no such thing as society', the idea that 'the bourgeois ideology of civil society is only an illusion' would have been particularly welcome. According to Negri, Spinoza allowed for no 'intermediate moment in the process that leads from the state of nature to the political state'.[10] Nature constructs individuals, and then, through cooperation, 'an infinite number of singularities are composed as productive essence'. The political is 'a multitude of cooperating singularities' co-extensive with the social but not mediated through it.[11] If civil society withers away, so much the better; the true structure of sovereignty is then laid bare.

Whether Hardt and Negri can manage without a more nuanced and autonomous conception of the social is another question, for in *Empire*, they take a rather different approach. Here, they object to social contract theorists who pretend 'that the subject can be understood presocially and outside the community and then impose a kind of transcendental socialization on it'.[12] The dialectic between the civil order and the natural order is now at an end, they argue, 'all phenomena and forces are artificial' and so 'no subjectivity is outside'. But if there is 'no more outside', how does that leave the claim that civil right is the aggregated power that individuals enjoy in the state of nature? Where there is no difference between the natural and the social, the distinction between the social and the political becomes all the more important. For what is the role of constituent power if sovereignty is always already constituted? Where now 'the Tartar who founds freedom in the experience of his own right'?

Ironically, one response to these questions may be found in Spinoza himself. It is not at all obvious that Negri's interpretation of Spinoza is correct. In the *Theologico-Political Treatise* Spinoza had maintained that some sort of social contract was necessary and that natural right was transferred. In the *Political Treatise*, the contract disappears, but whether the elimination of the contract means the continuation of natural right in the civil state or the elision of the difference between the civil and the natural is less certain. Spinoza sometimes says the former, but he also emphasizes that in the state of nature 'human natural right or freedom is a nonentity . . . [that] exists in imagination rather than fact, since there is no certainty of making it good'. Only on entering the commonwealth does natural right become more than a fiction: 'men in the state of nature can hardly be possessed of their own right'.[13] On this interpretation, civil right is the only form of right there is; in the state of nature there is so much risk that men are virtually powerless; far from taking their unalienated power into the commonwealth, men experience it there for the first time. For man, the social animal, if not for God or nature, *potestas* creates *potentia*.

The possible political consequences of this view were set out by John C. Calhoun, the Southern apologist for slavery whom Eugene Genovese termed 'the Marx of the Master Class'. He too vigorously affirmed the primacy of constituent power while denying that man could live in the natural state. According to Negri, Calhoun allows constituent power to reappear 'in its originary form' and take the shape of 'permanent revolution'.[14] But there is a catch. If, as Calhoun claims, man's 'natural state is the social and political', it suggests that 'instead of being born free and equal, [men] are born subject, not only to parental authority, but to the laws and institutions of the country'.[15] Constituent power is therefore essentially conservative in that it reflects the existing social order and the established interests of every group within it – the interests of slaveholders *qua* slaveholders, for example. To point out that Calhoun's theory of constituent power was developed in the service of a slave order is not 'ridiculous and hypocritical' as Negri claims. Calhoun's Tartar experiences his right in the ownership of slaves; the freedom he founds can never be theirs.

In order to avoid the implication that the constituent principle favours those who are already powerful Hardt and Negri have to reconcile the idea that 'there is no more outside' with the belief that 'constituent power comes from a void and constituents everything'.[16] The issue remains unresolved, but they seem to want to argue that the void is now on the inside because capitalism has, in effect, produced, a socially constructed state of nature. Hardt puts it in Deleuzian terms: 'One might interpret the crisis of the factory, the family, the church, and the other social enclosures as the progressive crumbling of various social walls that subsequently leave a social void, as if the striated social space of civil society has been smoothed into a vacant free space.'[17] Yet this void is filled with power. Using Foucault's concept of bio-power, Hardt and Negri argue that society is subsumed within power to the extent that 'the whole social body is comprised by power's machine'. Now, as in the state of nature, power constitutes society, not the other way round: 'Power, as it produces, organizes; as it organizes, it speaks and expresses itself as authority.'[18] Whether Foucault's biopolitics yields an adequate sociology of power is an open question. But leaving that aside, there are limitations to the kind of social formations the constituent principle can generate. Constituent power is produced by consensual rather than majoritarian decision, for if someone disagrees, they can just count themselves out. In *Insurgencies*, Negri makes no effort to disguise this, arguing that 'the strength of multitude . . . is always conceived . . . in the figure of the unity of the multitude'. Constituent power therefore has an elective affinity with forms of social solidarity in which agreement is essential. Its orientation is 'toward more and more communitarian configurations of life', for 'the desire for community is the spirit and soul of constituent power'.[19]

But the need for consensus is liable to limit the numbers involved. The centripetal dynamic of the constituent principle works better for small republics than for empires or even for counter-empires. What if the 'new nomad horde' of the multitude proves to be rather small? To this problem Hardt and Negri have no clear answer. In reply to Machiavelli's observation that the project of constructing a new society needs arms and money, they cite Spinoza and ask: 'Don't we already possess them? Don't the necessary weapons reside precisely within the creative and prophetic power of the multitude?'[20] No one is powerless; even the old, the sick, and the unemployed are engaged in the 'immaterial labour' that produces 'total social capital', and so, paradoxically: 'The poor itself is power. There is World Poverty, but there is above all World Possibility, and only the poor is capable of this.'[21]

It is difficult to see how this analysis comprehends the reality of powerlessness. You may be able to threaten the world with a Stanley knife (as the hijackers did so effectively on September 11, 2001), but you cannot build a new society with one. Insofar as the problems of the powerless have been addressed in recent years it is often through a dynamic that works in the opposite direction to the one Hardt and Negri suggest. Their response to globalization is to maintain that, since we have not contracted into global society, we still have all the power we need to change it. The alternative is to argue that a geographically boundless society must also be a totally inclusive society. The latter, of course, is an extension of what used to be called the politics of recognition. Globalization may have replaced multiculturalism as the focus of contemporary political debate, but there is an underlying continuity: the concern of anti-globalization protesters with remote regions of the world, with the lives of people unlike themselves, and with species of animals and plants that most have seen only on television is predicated on an unparalleled imaginative identification with the Other. This totalization of the politics of recognition from the local to the global is what has given momentum to campaigns such as the one for African AIDS victims; here, it is a question of sympathy rather than sovereignty, of justice rather than power. In many cases, unless the powerful recognized some kinship with them, the powerless would just die. Capitalism has no need for the 'immaterial labour' of millions now living. For powerless human beings, as for other species, autonomy leads to extinction.

The conflict at the centre of the movement against global capitalism is the tension between its libertarian stance and the demand for global justice. Although Hardt and Negri are pro-globalization and anti-capitalism they belong firmly in the libertarian camp. The 'postmodern republicanism' they advocate expresses the 'multitude's desire for liberation' through 'desertion, exodus, and nomadism'.[22] And although in *Kairòs, Alma Venus, Multitudo*, Negri has penned a series of meditations on poverty almost Franciscan in tone, the political theory he has developed over the past twenty years lacks the tools to deal with it. The assertion that the political is identical with the social cannot disguise the fact that his is a theory conceived entirely in terms of the former. As Hannah Arendt once noted approvingly of the American Revolution, this is a fight 'against tyranny and oppression, not against exploitation and poverty'.[23] For Arendt, it was the other sort of revolution, motivated by compassion rather than the desire for freedom, that led inexorably to terror and totalitarianism. She may not have been altogether wrong. Even the much-touted idea of a Tobin tax on currency speculation (designed to reduce market volatility and provide resources for sustainable development) would require worldwide ideological consensus for its enactment. Chasing foreign exchange trading from one tax haven to another, and from currency deals to bonds to commodities to derivatives needs bigger government than anything that currently exists. Effective environmental regulation would restrict the movement, fertility, and consumption-patterns of individuals all over the planet. The ideological alternative to neo-liberalism is, as neo-liberals never tire of saying, some form of totalitarianism.

But that can only be a reason for people to start thinking about what new forms of totalitarianism might be possible, and, indeed, desirable. In the United States, the discussion has been kick-started by the recent hijackings. Globalization appears to have created a world of unlimited risk, without a corresponding tota-lization of the means of social control. Some commentators, following Samuel P. Huntington's 'clash of civilizations' model, argue that global social control is impossible and the only way to contain risk is to maintain the boundaries between civilizations. For neo-liberals, however, commitment to globalization necessi-tates the search for some form of international authority. Yet this is unlikely to yield the type of intensive social regulation needed to limit all the risks of a global society. Unlimited risks need total controls, and, as Hardt and Negri pointed out, 'totalitarianism consists not simply in totalizing the effects of social life and subordinating them to a global disciplinary norm' but also in 'the organic foundation and unified source of society and the state'.[24]

Hardt and Negri have no interest in the control of risk – a world of unlimited risk is a world of unlimited constituent power – and they dismiss the totalitarian understanding of society as one in which 'community is not a dynamic collective creation but a primordial founding myth'. But the debate about social control prompted by the hijackings is one that others on the left should hurry to join. Without yet realizing it, the world's only superpower wants to achieve something that presupposes greater economic and social justice. Current US policy may be unacceptable, but the long-term project holds an unexpected promise, for if the 'war against terrorism' is going to be less of a fiasco than the 'war on drugs', it will require global social inclusivity and reciprocity.

Total social control involves a degree of microregulation with which individuals have to cooperate. One way in which totalitarian societies have differed from those that are merely authoritarian is in their provision of welfare and healthcare. (If you want to keep track of people you cannot abandon them when they are unemployed or sick.) The link between welfare and totalitarianism works both ways: social regulation and inclusion go together. If the United States wants to make the world a safer place, it will eventually have to offer, or force other governments to provide, the population of the entire world with the means to participate in a global society. This will involve real constraints on the operation of the market, particularly finance capital. September 11, 2001 may prove to be the date at which neo-liberalism and globalization began to part company.

'Nous sommes tous Américains', proclaimed the editorial in *Le Monde* a few days after the hijackings. And not just those who were horrified by them: the attack on New York and Washington was not an act of war against a foreign enemy (it had no strategic value) but a protest that implicitly acknowledged the sovereignty of the United States. 'I am an American Airlines pilot', boasted one hijacker, drinking in his local bar. A mix of black humour and wishful thinking no doubt, but a clear indication of psychological proximity. If Americans fail to understand why their country is hated, it is often because they barely comprehend the extent of its influence. No-one travels half way round the world to kill themselves amidst a people with whom they feel no connection. The 'clash of civilizations' approach fails to acknowledge the extent to which opposition to America is generated through imaginative identification with it. September 11, 2001 was the flip-side of the politics of recognition – another attempt to rebalance an internalized relationship with the Other. For the United States, the 'war on terrorism' may seem like a foreign war, but on the other side it is more like a civil war, dividing families – the bin Ladens, for instance.

One thing that the hijackings have brought to the surface is the extent to which 'the primordial founding myth' of a total society is already available in the history of the United States. At one level, Hardt and Negri recognize this. Their work is free of the European left's residual anti-Americanism and represents a systematic effort to appropriate the American myth for the global multitude. By arguing that imperial sovereignty is the US Constitution writ large, they manage to reinterpret global politics in terms of the American dialectic between the constituent and constitutional principles. This move may have helped the reception of *Empire* in the US, but it also condemns the multitude to repeat the mistake of the American left which, from the syndicalist unions of the early twentieth century to the New Left of the 1960s, persistently imagined that *potentia* would win out over *potestas* and was almost always proved wrong.

If the history of dissent in the United States shows anything it is surely that making power is no substitute for taking power. But just as the American left tried to disregard the role of the state, Hardt and Negri seek to minimize the role of the United States within the world. Indeed, it is one of their central contentions that 'The United States does not ... form the center of an imperialist project'.[25] Despite the extraordinary reach of American military, economic, and cultural power, Hardt and Negri maintain that global sovereignty is enjoyed not by the one nation with an acknowledged monopoly of violence, but by the nebulous Empire that the multitude has somehow 'called into being'. Here the theoretical limitations of their work constitute a strategic blindspot. During the past half century the United States has defeated socialism not just within America but all over the world. At the same time, the international left's few successes – decolonization, anti-racism, the women's movement – have all had the benefit of American support. At present, the United States is the only body with the capacity to realize the goals of the anti-globalization movement; without its backing, Tobin taxes and environmental regulation will come to nothing.

Hardt and Negri's acceptance of the American myth of limitless *potentia* does not deal with the reality of American *potestas*, it simply ignores it. They miss the point that even if the multitude could create its own Americas, it would still have to deal with the existing one. Within the current conjuncture, to take power is to take America. Any global political project which does not make this its objective is barely credible. The United States may not be a utopia, but a utopian politics now has to be routed through it. And it is not impossible, for the US remains permeable. It is a young nation with relatively porous borders, an egalitarian ethos, and a democratic tradition; more states may one day join the

Union. For both individuals and countries, accepting *de jure* as well as *de facto* American sovereignty may eventually prove to be the best means of promoting political change. As the 'war against terrorism' has made clear, a US administration that is minutely responsive to shifts in domestic opinion can afford to remain indifferent to even its most powerful allies. We may all be Americans now, but we are not all citizens, and not to be a US citizen is to be globally disenfranchised.

The failure of the left to come to terms with America is, in large part, a legacy of the Cold War. While the Soviet Union still existed it was rational to suppose that human emancipation might be effected, if only indirectly, through the leverage of the Communist bloc. To this project the US constituted an obstacle. But there is now no geo-political reason why America should not be transformed into the vehicle of those aspirations to which it once stood opposed. Indeed, in some respects the US is better suited to the role than the Soviet Union ever was. The USSR, like other totalitarian regimes, got a bad name less because of its monopolistic control of everyday life than on account of its stifling insistence on a maximum of shared values, and its draconian punishments for nonconformity. Twentieth-century totalitarianisms were, in Durkheimian terms, attempts to create total communities rather than total societies. The United States offers a model for a different type of totalitarianism.

Tocqueville was perhaps the first to describe its features. Noting that as 'the conditions of men become equal among a people, individuals seem of less and society of greater importance', he linked the egalitarian atomization of American life not only to the dominance of the social over the communal, but also to the centralized power of the state: each man 'is a stranger to the fate of all the rest . . . he is close to them, but he does not see them; he touches them but he does not feel them', while above him 'stands an immense and tutelary power . . . absolute, minute, regular, provident, and mild'. The two feed off one another, for central power naturally 'encourages the principle of equality' and equality 'facilitates, extends, and secures the influence of a central power'.[26]

Although Tocqueville presents this coupling of equality and central power as the source of a new form of tyranny in which people will be infantilized by the state, an egalitarian can only regret that America failed to develop in the way he envisaged. Within a total society – a world of universal *anomie* populated by the hybridized subjects of mutual recognition – monopolistic microregulation need not be concerned with conformity. Of course, a global United States is not a total society, but total society is rapidly becoming more imaginable than the state of nature from which political theorizing has traditionally started. In this situation we need to start thinking in new ways. Negri's version of what Althusser called 'totality without closure' is a politics without a social contract, 'a constituent power without limitations'.[27] But in a total society, it is not the social that needs a contract but the individual – an anti-social contract that creates individual spaces in a world totally regulated by meaningless mutuality.

Notes

1. Antonio Negri, *The Savage Anomaly*, trans. Michael Hardt, Minneapolis 1991, p. 195.
2. Antonio Negro, *Insurgencies: Constituent Power and the Modern State*, trans. M. Boscagli, Minneapolis 1999, p. 146.
3. Ibid., p. 206 and p. 2.
4. Michael Hardt and Antonio Negri, *Empire*, Cambridge MA: Harvard University Press 2000, p. xii.
5. Ibid., p. xv.
6. Ibid., p. 44.
7. *Insurgencies*, p. 181.
8. *Empire*, p. 349.
9. *Insurgencies*, pp. 148–9.
10. *The Savage Anomaly*, p. 200.
11. *Insurgencies*, pp. 332 and 333.
12. *Empire*, p. 353.
13. Benedict de Spinoza, *Political Works*, trans. A. G. Wernham, Oxford 1958, p. 277 (*Tractatus Politicus*, II.15).
14. *Insurgencies*, pp. 186–7.
15. John C. Calhoun, *A Disquisition on Government*, in *Works*, New York 1863, vol. 1, p. 58.
16. *Insurgencies*, p. 16.
17. Michael Hardt, 'The Withering of Civil Society', *Social Text*, 45 (1995), p. 35.
18. *Empire*, p. 24 and p. 33.
19. *Insurgencies*, pp. 308 and 323, and 23.
20. *Empire*, p. 65.
21. Ibid., p. 157.
22. Ibid., p. 210.

23. H. Arendt, *On Revolution*, London 1964, p. 68.
24. *Empire*, p. 113.
25. Ibid., p. xiv.
26. Alexis de Tocqueville, *Democracy in America*, Ware 1998, pp. 344, 358, and 349.
27. *Insurgencies*, p. 25.

The Italian Ideology

Timothy Brennan

> Possibility, seriously considered ... is not what with luck
> might happen. It is what we can believe in enough to want,
> and then, by active wanting, make possible. ... [A]fter
> defeats and failures, and both within and after certain
> profound disillusions, it is not recovery or return but direct
> practical possibility. ... Possibility as a different order,
> which no longer from simple assumptions, or from known
> discontents and negations, but on our own responsibility,
> in an actual world, we must prove.
>
> – Raymond Williams (1980)[1]

Antonio Negri and Michael Hardt's *Empire*, whatever else one
makes of it, is an opportunely titled book. Emblazoned across its
cover is the first of many wordplays whose purpose is to enact a
kind of productive ambiguity. It works by appropriating the
charge of the very problem it seeks to bypass, even surpass. For
Empire, it turns out, has almost nothing to say about the historical
legacy of imperialsim. There are, of course, discussions of the
'end of colonialism', of the effects of the Vietnam War on the
American government and European youth, on the disasters of
the 'nation' for the anti-colonial movements; and there are several
vignettes of postcolonial identity (on Toussaint L'Ouverture, for
example) and references to Marx's writing on India, as well as
Sartre's essays on race. But the colonized of today are given little
place in the book's sprawling theses on multitudes, the subjectivity
of labour, biopolitical control, and the creation of alternative

values. This radical elision perhaps tells us something about the book's own value hierarchy as well as the kind of audience it wishes to reach with its propositions on behalf of 'organi[zing] the multitude'.[2]

It cannot be said that *Empire* is indifferent to the religious/ ethnic missionary zeal of the classical and modern empires themselves. But the authors' focus is never on imperialism as an infrastructural necessity – of either capitalism or some other social force. What preoccupies them, by contrast, is the historical ambivalence of imperialism's various epistemes, where European conquest is seen as having been a utopian project. To put this another, but no less problematic, way: the main interest of imperialism for Hardt and Negri lies in the new forms of identity it has unleashed across the globe – a view that fits, *mutatis mutandis*, very comfortably with a mainstream perception that America's global influence has been largely positive. It would be difficult, even foolish, to separate *Empire*'s favourable coverage in the mainstream press from this aspect of its message.[3]

At the heart of Hardt and Negri's project are four basic arguments. First, that the age of imperialism has given way, under globalization, to a new age of 'Empire'; second, that a tradition of radical thought from Italy is uniquely situated to broker a wedding of Deleuzian theory with Marxist practice – the philosophical amalgam necessary for bringing Empire to recognition. Both propositions require, in turn, a third: an updated analysis of the new types and shifting parameters of post-industrial labour. It is here that one finds an attempt to portray a new 'subjectivity of labor' manifest in the 'multitude' – a social formation unprecedented in appearance and incalculable in importance, like Gramsci's subaltern in that it avoids an over-reliance on the analytic of class. Finally (and this is *Empire*'s most provocative gambit, and its only claim to originality), the revolution long sought by the left need not be planned or hoped for. It has already taken place.

Readers captivated by such far-reaching, even foundational, assertions are, however, immediately confronted by a dilemma. Why, just when American leaders have openly declared their imperial ambitions, is the end of imperialism confidently announced? And why by intellectuals on the far left for whom the older legacies of communism are *not radical enough*? The imperatives underlying these questions seem so contradictory, in fact, that one hunts for a dialectical mode capable of explaining how a deeply ambitious theoreticism – the full flower, in fact, of three decades of refined '68ist Continental philosophy – could come to sound, in *Empire*'s hands, so pragmatic, so cheery and, if one can put it this way, so *American*.[4]

The answers to these questions can be located in the fact that, as I shall argue, *Empire* embodies a deeply ambivalent left/right impulse derived from one of the theoretical legacies of the 1960s. I would also argue that we need a vocabulary for describing the inability within cultural theory to distinguish between resistance and conformity – an inability that defines the present climate of cultural theory itself.

Value and self-valorization

Let me turn to a closer examination of *Empire*'s conceptual apparatus. *Empire* is above all a *return*: a 'recapture', as Gilles Deleuze and Félix Guattari have put it in a very different context.[5] If we take only its most prominent themes, *Empire* reprises the globalization debates of the last two decades in fairly straightforward ways.[6] In its pages, readers again find the history of Bretton Woods, the routine treatments of the Treaty of Westphalia, the obligatory references to the British East India Company, and the birth of the Internet, all described in superfluous detail because they have been treated in any number of previously published books. Its turn to 'biopolitics' closely follows the arguments of Anthony Giddens' 'life political agenda' in writings from over a decade ago.[7] Moreover, the authors' basic premise is part of the stock-in-trade of earlier cosmo-theory: namely, that the age of imperialism has passed.[8] The great powers of old, we are again told, ruled in the name of single nations, whereas today we find a supranational entity that coheres without coherence and rules without government (Hardt and Negri's term is 'Empire,' but others have given this basic concept other names: 'the global ecumene' or, in a more critical variant, 'McWorld').

In its practical demands, moreover, Negri's work (in *Empire* as elsewhere) is indistinguishable from that of an earlier time. In many ways that work squarely fits within the traditions of council communism of Europe of the 1930s and 1940s, which rejected

programmatic political organization as dangerous and counterproductive, and placed its stress on spontaneous eruptions and
on a tactical orientation based on a rhetoric of 'given possibilities'. Like the council communists, Negri considers capitalism
so ubiquitous and penetrating it cannot be directly opposed;
workers must, by contrast, work inside it, finding their own 'mass
rhythm', basing their collectivity on 'social average labour time'
until they plan their own productivity.[9] Many of *Empire*'s arguments, in other words, attest to the ways that their formulation of
the 'new' was debated seven decades ago. At least some of the
admiration for the book depends on the sad historical fact that
the histories of the labour movement have become unfamiliar to
audiences, and so these latter-day echoes of that past appear
novel.

But to speak of *Empire* as a return is also a way of alluding to its
emergence from a *new Italian* political tradition – its having grown
out of a milieu provided by the *autonomia* movements of the
Italian far left of the 1970s, whose theorists have lately presented
themselves publicly as a 'front': the descendants of earlier street
clashes now seasoned by the sophistications of Franco-German
theory.[10] *Empire* is a new Italian text, in that sense, and must be
seen within that constellation. It should be remembered that
Hardt and Negri stress these national-cultural associations *themselves*; that is, they repeatedly draw our attention to the specifically
Italian radicalism they espouse, the particular advantages of coming to politics in what Hardt and Paolo Virno call 'laboratory
Italy', and the public existence of the 'front' that constitutes, in
their terms, a new 'Italian radical thought' as such.[11]

Like that earlier impossible unity 'French Theory', new Italian
thought involves an orientation to a national past, an intellectual
corpus, and – above all – to an instinctive understanding of the
strength in numbers that comes from a national-cultural identity.
This is an important feature of the purported globalism Hardt
and Negri say they represent; as in so many other instances of
globalization, the national-cultural retains its force, and enables
the very discourse that veils its continued existence. Italy's periph-
eral place in Europe's South, its notoriously weak and short-lived
postwar governments and its hothouse radicalizations of the 1970s
have all coalesced in an image of a corresponding theoretical
fermentation. A new Italian theory reinvigorates its earlier French

counterpart, taking over in the wake of lagging French energies and the fatigue of its intellectual stereotypes.[12]

The portrait of economic change offered by Hardt and Negri bears a striking resemblance to the sort of analysis routinely offered by *The Economist* and the *Wall Street Journal*: namely, that capitalism has abruptly realigned its economic priorities in favour of the intellectual component in formerly manual work, a process to which the new Italians assign the term 'immaterial labor'. The language of management theory has for over a decade bulged with a figural repertoire demoting sweat and muscle in favour of 'skills', 'insights', 'ideas', and 'speed.' It is now little more than a cliché of the management genre. And yet, apart from the belatedness of 'discovering' this largely fictional fact about the new economy, this is a scenario that *Empire*'s authors do not merely lament. Rather like the columnists of the business press, they are encouraged by a systemic shift that makes them optimistic (in much the way that in the early 1990s the post-Fordist critics of 'New Times' discussed the oppositional potential of consumption and the attendant subversiveness of the decentering introduced by niche marketing).[13] While enlivening its terminologies by placing them in new philosophical registers, the authors' devotion to New Times credos is unwavering.[14]

But let us note (contra the New Times/New Labour, new global order enthusiasts) that it takes no specialist to recognize that manufacture has been 'informationalized'. This is common knowledge. It is quite another thing, however, to pose this informatization as an exhilarating sign of the sophistications of capitalism as it frees up the biopolitical sphere while facilitating the 'refusal of work'; and then to further portray it as an *anagoge* of high theory performing its grand conceptual tasks. This romantic view prevents readers from noticing how the aura of such thinking in practice mystifies the reality of globalization, which is a vast enterprise set up to encourage capital mobility while domesticating labour.

A great leap of the imagination, therefore, is demanded in order to grapple with *Empire*'s diagnosis. We enter a controlled environment of the 'as if,' a primarily subjunctive horizon. The book's ethical utopia immortalizes precisely what is weakest in Marx's work while attacking Marx's strengths – his vivid descriptions of the logic of capital and the human toll it takes. If the

Marx who wrote of 'communism' as a utopian outcome is the least convincing Marx, it is the only one Hardt and Negri retain.

What unfolds in *Empire* more successfully than in Negri's earlier books is the development of a rhetoric of ambivalence designed to suture the worlds of Sorelian workerism (accented with references to a more explicitly Marxist revolutionary tradition) and 1960s counterculturalism: the mapped territory, in other words, of Negri's divided origins. To this end, the book's slogan, 'the refusal of work', for instance (taken originally from Mario Tronti), is crafted to evoke the strike, the slowdown, or industrial sabotage, on the one hand, and on the other, an anti-authoritarian 'dropping out' – a rejection of the work-a-day rhythms and disciplines of 'voluntary servitude'.[15] However, in Hardt and Negri's usage it means neither exactly. As Tronti, a lifetime member of the Communist Party of Italy (PCI), had developed the idea in his highly influential *Operai e capitale* (1966), the capitalist is the one, paradoxically, who provides labour while the worker provides capital, not the other way around.[16] The 'refusal of work', then, is for Tronti a revolutionary opting-out of the perpetual cycle of the transformation of labour into surplus-value rather than a merely temporary stoppage of productive relations as takes place in a typical strike.[17] The original move by Tronti was a bold attempt to remind labourers of their power in the context of organizational struggle, and to attack the very underlying logic of the relationship of commodity production in order to push organized labour beyond the mere search for a better deal. In the hands of new Italian thought exemplified by Hardt and Negri, refusal becomes a substitute for organization.

Readers of *Empire* may not be aware of the genesis of its underlying economic ideas or their development over the span of Negri's *oeuvre* in dialogue with his new Italian compatriots. For Negri as for the other new Italians, escaping the regimentation of a job (that is, not 'selling out' in its 1960s sense) undermines capitalism itself. As a result, politics can henceforth be based on forms of non-involvement and insubordination rather than on alliances or agendas. Practice too can be a deliberate non-practice safeguarded by inaction from the taint of an unseemly power. Invoking mass insubordination as a principle – the refusal of work – *Empire* strives to escape the merely circular trade-offs and inversions of power politics and sees itself as delving into the very foundations of political motive: replacing the principle of material interest with that of 'desire'. Postulated as being more fundamental, desire is for them more radically enabling, more an absolute precondition of activity.

As early as the 1990s, new Italian theorists such as Paolo Virno had transmuted this duality of politics and power into a purified 'will to be against'.[18] This 'will' as new Italian thinking presented it, was poised not only against the state but also the traditional parties and trade unions. 'Immaterial labor', another transitional theme, at first seems to signal nothing more than a reference to the symbolic analysts of the information economy as they have been described by former Clinton labour secretary Robert Reich, Anthony Giddens, and others.[19] In their own account, Hardt and Negri do little to extend the term, and they are quite open about its having no special meaning. Just as it suggests in the work of Reich, for instance, it refers in *Empire* to labour that 'produces an immaterial good, such as a service, a cultural product, knowledge, or communication'.[20]

Immaterial labour has enormous ambitions within new Italian thought generally, and to review the course of its elaboration clarifies its role in Hardt and Negri's book. In Virno and Hardt's *Radical Thought in Italy*, for example, Maurizio Lazzarato claims that the term explodes the concept of labour by focusing on its cultural content, a form of labour that 'defin[es] and fix[es] cultural and artistic standards, fashions, tastes, consumer norms, and, more strategically, public opinion.'[21] Both in this text and in *Empire*, an older sense of countercultural street wisdom blends with a reverence for a much more traditional exegesis of texts from classical Marxism. Such nods to traditionalism, even orthodoxy, represent a highly significant manoeuvre in new Italian thinking, which feels compelled to claim a continuity and rigour it does not possess. Hardt and Negri, like other new Italian thinkers, live in a world of divided sentiments, morbidly obsessed with the rhetorical gestures of early Marxist parties and struggles (indeed, unable to slough off their inspirations) while driven by the antagonistic counter-logics of 'theory' which is allergic to battles of this older type.

This peculiar juggling of sources allows all three to make crucial claims for their redefinition of politics, and it is important to understand how this relationship to the past works. Virno, for example, argues that Marx asserts that abstract knowledge becomes 'precisely by virtue of its autonomy from production, nothing less than the principal productive force'.[22] And yet, were one to approach the *Grundrisse* outside this carefully prepared rhetorical frame, it would be very difficult to find anything in Marx that attested to such a hypostatization of thought. The passage of the *Grundrisse* to which Hardt and Negri refer is about the contradiction inherent in the creation of surplus free time by mechanization. Marx points out that this process poses a problem for capitalists who wish to turn free time into surplus labour. So when Marx alludes to the 'general intellectual' – which in the original is a passing phrase rather than a major category – he makes clear that he is speaking of the role of industrial planning ('intellect') in increasing the ratio of fixed to variable capital. In other words, there is no hint that Marx equates managerial planning with theoretical inquiry as such, much less that he projects a future in which immaterial values displace basic production as the motor of capitalist profit-making. The *Grundrisse* sets out to describe how the clerical abstractions of gifted statesman educators and political economists (Marx's 'theorists') would become more and more important as capitalism progressed, not – as Hardt and Negri argue (echoing Reich) – that knowledge would become the primary productive force.

For Hardt and Negri, the 'general intellect' is both a threat and a promise (much as it is for Reich) in a sense similar to the way in which Empire is both a system of command from above and a potential structure of popular will. Capitalism may be tough, they imply, but it is good. Computerization, for instance, apart from being an enticing technological innovation (the 'new') may have the negative appearance of helping management normalize the work of labourers – standardizing and disciplining their behaviours. And yet, at the same time, it represents the 'liberation of living labor' for it relies on the 'constellation of powerful singularities'. Hardt and Negri put the same idea in another way as well: capital creates an 'open space' in which the subject can constitute 'a new position of being'.[23] Instead of swallowing up subjectivity within production, making 'the total person part of the process,' capitalism creates 'a polymorphous, self-employed, autonomous work . . . a kind of 'intellectual worker' who is him- or herself an entrepreneur'.[24]

One might at first take the word 'entrepreneur' to be an ironic reference to that excess produced by capitalism that is, for Hardt and Negri, a specific grounds for optimism: the contradiction left to exploit. The dialectical notion here would then be that capitalism produces a re-empowered subject who is better able to resist the regimentation forced on him/her in the name of productivity. On the other hand, one might see this gesture as not in the least ironic. It would then appear to be an enthusiastic admission that capitalism's emphasis on the sacrosanct individual should be communism's emphasis as well. The part of Negri's work that forms the basis of *Empire*'s economic theory strongly suggests that the latter option is more strongly inflected. His effort is to 'invert praxis' in the frame of the current form of value, insisting (and trying to make us see) that the political and the social are indistinguishable, that the social is day-to-day life, just living. As such, revolutionary practice is really just a matter of being as well as possessing what he rather theatrically calls a 'radically, ontologically autonomous' consciousness.[25]

The focus of new capitalism on *personality* creates the conditions for a 'silent revolution'. To put this another way, the ' "raw material" of immaterial labour is subjectivity',[26] and therefore capital's international tensions express themselves in a strengthening of the liberated individual in a happily chaotic network of other individuals forming *Empire*'s multitude: 'New figures of struggle and new subjectivities are produced in the conjuncture of events, in the universal nomadism, in the general mixture and miscegenation of individuals and populations, and in the technological metamorphoses of the imperial biopolitical machine'.[27, 28] The most intense radicalism (that which pushes beyond mere needs to the irreducible 'cell' of biological desire) finds its refuge and answer in capitalism itself, the sources of a revolution more radical than mere *ressentiment.*

Unlike Foucault, therefore, who regarded governments as evolving from cloddy 'discipline' to a more subtle and pernicious 'control,' Hardt and Negri echo that radical thinker of our times, *New York Times* op. ed. columnist Thomas Friedman, in contending that people have lately increased their options for self-definition:

> Empire's rule has no limits. . . . [It] posits a regime that effectively encompasses the spatial totality . . . an order that effectively suspends

history and thereby fixes the existing state of affairs for eternity . . . operates on all registers of the social order extending down to the depths of the social world. . . . Power cannot mediate among different social forces, it rather creates a new milieu of maximum plurality and uncontainable singularization.[29]

For Hardt and Negri the march of the juggernaut – as ominous as it is anonymous – is at the same time the victory march of the disorganized followers and witnesses of the new anti-regime who blend imperceptibly (and conveniently) into the regime itself. At one with neo-liberalism's fearful warnings of the seeping of the state into every crevice of society, the passage above conjures an irrepressible mass subject that conquers the state by virtue of capitalism's need for 'maximum plurality' – a gathering of subjectivities (the multitude) who never actually meet or converse, and who therefore can never be guilty of repressing their political foes or, for that matter, of exercising their political wills.

Central to *Empire*, then, is not just the notion that imperialism is passé, that nations are defunct, or that the United States has lost its hegemony. Indeed, these views – although demonstrably false – are held by significant wings of the mainstream social sciences and the business press, and are also hegemonic in globalization theory. What is new in *Empire* is its argument that working-class and student militancy from the 1960s and 1970s *created* globalization from below, and that capitalism co-opted its innovative forms of dissidence by mimicking them.[30] This astounding thesis is stated with insistent clarity (and, it should be said, in a revealingly theological tone): 'The multitude called Empire into being'.[31] How the unemployed, the de-skilled, the reified, the politically disenfranchized and the mercilessly propagandized accomplished this or, more to the point, why they did so, is a problem *Empire* never pretends to work out. Only the blanket equation of 'the state' with oppression could prompt the authors to confuse, as they routinely do, deregulation with emancipation, the centre with the periphery, and the IMF with the GPAs (that is, those 'Global Peoples Assemblies' that political scientists like Richard Falk and Andrew Strauss have been promoting as the only hope for a new international civil society).[32]

Consequently, despite an enormous apparatus of citation, *Empire* is simply unable to see the sharp historical differences between globalization and internationalism (the two are actually opposites), concluding that 'The decline of the nation-state shows that proletarian internationalism won'.[33, 34] Vigilant readers are forced to notice the enormous irony of all this. The very forces on which *Empire* draws and with which it identifies (council communism, post-Fordism, Deleuze and Guattari), all stand opposed to economism, positivism, and evolutionism – taken to be the untenably mechanistic legacies of Second International Marxism. But here are Hardt and Negri professing, in a particularly unguarded form, a mechanical/organic theory of inevitability.

Negri's prolific output over three decades might lead to the expectation that *Empire* is a *tour de force* of economic and traditional Marxist theory; that not only was his mastery of its older forms on display, but that he had creatively, even epochally, refashioned it. So given the decades of this apprenticeship, it is especially surprising to see a number of simple gaffes. One of the key rationalizations offered in *Empire*, for instance, is the conceptual monad of labour and labour power. Hardt and Negri have the habit of adducing labour power as an agent or subjectivity (as the worker him or herself).[35] But this appears to be a misprision, because the term traditionally refers to the commodity the worker sells – that separable entity of physical force whose usefulness has the unique property of creating exchange value. This is roughly analogous to confusing value with price, or profit with surplus value, as many casual readers of political economy are wont to do. It is contextually clear that the authors are not redefining tradition, only sloppy in their use of it.

In addition to errors, one is also confronted by unsupple interpretations which can, at times, lead to embarrassing oversights. Take, for example, the passage below, based on Deleuze and Guattari's concept of 'desiring production':

> Whereas 'outside measure' refers to the impossibility of power's calculating and ordering production at a global level, 'beyond measure' refers to the vitality of the productive context, the expression of labor as desire, and its capacities to constitute the bio-political fabric of Empire from below. Beyond measure refers to the new place in the non-place, the place defined by the productive activity that is autonomous from any external regime of measure. Beyond measure refers to a virtuality that invests the entire bio-political fabric of imperial

globalization. By the virtual we understand the set of powers to act (being, loving, transforming, creating) that reside in the multitude.[36]

But are not the available economic indicators (state budgets, the census, marketing projections) formidably detailed 'regimes of measure' designed precisely to address the desires of those who believe themselves 'autonomous' in order better to exploit an illusory 'choice'? Virtuality, similarly, can be understood in this passage only in a highly metaphoric way because corporate activity always unfolds in locatable (that is, non-virtual) countries, cities, or buildings.[37] As such, 'non-places' are not really non-places at all, except in that juridical sense so convenient to corporations in the act, say, of money-laundering, off-shore brokering, or escaping the white-collar crime unit of the FBI. Moreover, the 'productive context' evoked by the authors can only be that very desire they identify as the new reality of labour, whose power now resides in an intransitive being, loving, and self-transforming, at the expense of a concerted, disciplined anti-institutional agency. In the slippery syntactical constructions of the above passage, labour is desire, and yet (for this is how ambivalence works) the only labour that is desire is the authors' labour of desiring a new labor, which they rhetorically produce.[38] This writing, which typifies *Empire*, has the unintended effect of promoting the same legalistic and rhetorical legerdemain of capitalism's apologists.

The problem with the conceptual conflations has less to do perhaps with syntactical matters than it does with the fact that *Empire* operates in terms of an *interstitial* logic. It plays in the theoretical registers of plausible deniability. Readers favourably inclined to the book are quick to observe, for example, that it is not 'capital' the authors are talking about, but the *command* of capital, just as the focus is not on imperialism but a new 'system of command' called Empire that strives fruitlessly to discipline its mass creators while laying governments to waste, preparing the multitude for its rightful inheritance. Within this conceptual no-man's land (the *non-place* that is their *new place*), the authors can never be reproached for leaving out history, or for liquidating opposition by assuming their opponent's forms, since the ready riposte can always be that the reader has merely misunderstood; the commitments of meaning are by nature ambiguous in their strategy of 'indirection'. Presumably relegated to the status of

bogus proof-mongering, neither method nor supporting evidence
need detain one over the subtleties of *Empire* whose elaboration
lies in the construction of genealogies and periodizations and
calls primarily for a theoretical approach.
This fresco of the political constitution of the present renders
ambiguity the virtue of being 'theoretical'. The gains of such
confident superiority are that declarations can be made, then
qualified, with vague gestures and allusive generosity. It is not as
though its shimmering depiction of a deeply contradictory world
political reality is, as far as it goes, uninviting or without potential.
For, resistance should be versatile and should exploit the opportunities provided even by the power one opposes. So one can
appreciate Hardt and Negri's emphasis, at one point, that
'Empire' is not a metaphor but a *concept* – a living form that
structures. By the same token, this move comes with its own
obligations: a concept must have an object. *Empire*, however,
collapses in the passage from concept to object. To take one
example, the book counterintuitively argues that capitalism is
driven by a logic of 'renouncing pleasure'[39] – a view, that many of
capitalism's enthusiasts might find puzzling, since Madison
Avenue has for some time sold not only commodities but a system
of pleasure. Along these lines, it has been widely argued, for
instance, that the United States is rapidly becoming little more
than an 'entertainment economy.' But the authors are driven to
the anachronistic Weberian notion of protestant restraint by an
identitarian logic that they never question, or even foresee as a
problem. Conversely, the leisure that follows from the 'refusal of
work' becomes a realm of potential pleasure, and expresses itself
in the following way: 'autonomy' is that process in which labour
does not produce value in manufacture but rather 'valorizes
itself'.[40] Economics, then, is tantamount to a 'revaluation of
values' and *Empire*'s 'revolution' is the worker at leisure who is
himself valuable *for being able to redefine 'value'*. The tautology is
again imposed.
   If, however, the blows to the meaningful agency of the worker
as subject, and to his/her critical placement in production, are
consequential, they are less so than the book's concealing of the
intellectual as agent.[41] For an important aspect of new Italian
thought is its well-prepared refusal to reckon with the destructive
potential of the theorist's own prognoses that might, at least in

principle, be the result of exaggerating the importance of 'mass intellectuality' and the 'general intellect.' An economy of the type Hardt and Negri describe would seem to demand an investigation of the intellectual at work – itself a prototype of immaterial labour, and perhaps its most obvious commodity. But even while dwelling on the self, the new Italians are strangely silent about the mode of the self when it comes to their theory's immediate beneficiaries. Empire, say Hardt and Negri, is 'autopoietic.' Aside from this word's evolutionist tinges, the view denies the agency of intellectuals in making theory. What Hardt and Negri diagnose as the dissipation of labour (or rather its erasure by way of a generalization into all spheres) is rather an echo of their own estrangement from labour.

Since the 'system' for Hardt and Negri 'constructs social fabrics that evacuate or render ineffective any contradiction . . . in an insignificant play of self-generating and self-regulating equilibria',[42] it is logical for them to conclude that the only true agency must occur within subjectivity, which is located in social fabrics but not of them. The end of labor can then be announced as though it were a vast expansion of types of labour. The reader hears about atomized constituencies, the ensemble of social forces, the atmospheric penetration of power into all spheres, but nothing of the effects of law and obligation on organization or the capacity to learn. As a result, the authors' advocacy for a post-organizational 'line of flight' towards the general intellect appears merely as intellectual flight. In other words, the 'new sovereignty' they speak of is indistinguishable from an evacuation of personnel in the sense that, robbed of the hope of making or changing anything by exertion or plan, intellectuals effect the very negative outcomes described as the original premise of their turn. The conditions to which they point when declaring the need for a theoretical rupture with the telos, and conceptual modalities, of the past, are the conditions *they helped create* by a mesmerizing diagnosis laid out in advance. At the end, the economic theory of new Italian thought is not an economics at all. At best, it is a poetics aimed at revising the meaning of the circuitry of production into the management of the self: an antediluvian *oikos*. '*Self-valorization*' thus implies an attempt to change the game of politics and economics in a redrawing of the field of battle. One wins, but only by redefining what victory means.

Assemblage

For a rigorous reading, it is not enough to admire *Empire*'s verbal intensity and verve, or remark on the mnemonic effects of its cheeky coinages and sweeping rhythms. If the book's success is tightly bound to its rhetorical performance, there are nevertheless methodological issues embedded in the project that transcend what is normally called 'style.' *Empire*'s modes of telling are at least as important as its tale because of the way the authors symptomatically repeat gestures that have become almost automatic in contemporary cultural theory. For what first strikes one about the project is its deeply incommensurable enlistment of theoretical precursors in the name of interdisciplinarity whose frank utilitarianism reveals itself methodologically as 'assemblage'.[43]

Assemblage, a term taken from *A Thousand Plateaus*, refers to a methodological eclecticism Deleuze and Guattari counterpose to science. It expresses itself as a gathering of substantively incompatible positions. In *Empire*'s assemblage, the juxtaposition of figures whose political views are mutually hostile to one another (Spinoza and Machiavelli, for instance, or Schmitt and Gramsci) is presented as the supersession of earlier divisions in pursuit of a more supple and inclusive combination. A less exacting process of distinctions can in this way pass itself off as a more inventive, less sectarian vision. Ventriloquizing the traditions of Marxist theory, Hardt and Negri reappropriate them in a more contemporary and, they would argue, more relevant way; but as with all commodities under the triumph of exchange-value, the principle that matters most to them is equivalence. This style of argumentation, in fact, was already familiar to Theodor Adorno, who in 1957 condemned it as the 'neutralization of culture':

> The neutralization of culture ... indicates a more or less general reflection on the fact that intellectual formations have lost their bindingness, because they have detached themselves from any possible relationship to social praxis and become ... objects of purely mental apprehension. ... They become cultural commodities exhibited in a secular pantheon in which contradictory entities – works that would like to strike each other dead – are given space side-by-side in a false pacification: Kant and Nietzsche, Bismark and Marx, Clemens Brentano and Büchner. This waxworks of great men then finally confesses

its desolation in the uncounted and unconsidered images in every museum, in the editions of classics in covetously locked bookcases.[44]

The counterpart to assemblage in a formal sense is that ensemble of social forces in whom Hardt and Negri place their political faith – those disparate, atomized constituencies that correspond to the interests of no class or faction ('new constellations' in their terms). The parallel between the level of form and content is achieved by drawing on Spinoza – the great counter-Hegel of their neo-Marxism. Spinoza provides the authors with their putatively materialist, counter-dialectical mantra: 'immanence'. The problem with employing Spinoza for this purpose, however, is that his *immanence*, like their own, is oddly *transcendent*. In Spinoza himself there is a fundamental ambiguity about whether identifying God with the present materiality of nature outwits theology, transforming it cleverly into a materialism before its time; or whether it only reduces the material to the mere permeating presence of God.[45] As Howard Kainz puts it while neatly summarizing Hegel's view of Spinoza: 'there is too much God, so that man and the world are reduced to nothing'.[46] Much in the manner of Spinoza's Ethics, one proceeds in *Empire* by way of a geometrical ordering, a system of axioms as though compensating with figural rigidity for a situation in which intuitive knowledge stands in for evidence, and freedom is a largely intellectual achievement.

The book's 'new constellations' appear little more, finally, than philosophical organs ripped out of their original systems and rendered meaningless except as a declaration of the authors' habits of reading. To be accused simply of eclecticism would not, of course, bother Hardt and Negri per se, for they have responded dismissively in the past to this charge as if implying that their accusers were simply scandalized by the heresy of their amalgam and had failed to see the novelty of their *combinatoire*.[47] Notwithstanding the authors' special pleading, the problem with assemblage is, at base, epistemological. How does one borrow ideas without assuming their contextual resonances as first formulated in a system, regardless of whether such a system is summoned for contemporary use? Because Hardt and Negri ignore this logical difficulty, they have little choice but to revert to a *functional* relationship to the concepts they adduce. As such, their 'new constellations' are rendered vulgarly pragmatic; they represent an idealist utilitarianism, justified in the name of that wholly American thing, a 'toolbox'.[48]

If a discrete idea can be wrenched from its whole so that now it becomes the new autonomous whole, then one has to entertain the possibility that the resulting mélange might, at least in principle, be incoherent.[49] Even if one wanted to defend an argument-by-amalgam for its power to create novel constellations, one would have to recognize the distinct risk of devising a *false* assemblage. But Hardt and Negri appear not to have considered this possibility. Far from being an emergent or radical Deleuzian methodological politics, eclecticism is the reverse coin of hegemonic cultural theory. By this light, assemblage appears to be the principal use-value allowing the critic rapidly to shift thinkers, positions, and terminologies in order to play to a segmented or globally-commodified audience of bohemians-in-training.

This can-do relationship to the archive made fashionable – because all ages, figures, and traditions are available for immediate use – gives *Empire*'s writing an aura of the eternal present even as it comfortably fits the American reader's pragmatist political unconscious. But this present poses as the future and is informed, as I have suggested, by an unacknowledged (and often misunderstood) past. My earlier depiction of *Empire* as a recapture, therefore, revisits the argument about assemblage as a mode of argumentation. For *Empire*'s nomadology is indeed what Deleuze and Guattari call it: 'the opposite of history'.[50] Still, given the reverential nod of the book towards an old-left organizational past (Rosa Luxemburg in particular is deployed to this effect), Hardt and Negri want to historicize all the same, and much of *Empire* is written in a frankly historicist mode. What they lack, however, is any sense of what Raymond Williams called the 'residual.' *Empire*'s paradoxical return is a rushing towards one's past, while being unable to face another. Or, to put it differently, there is no feel in this writing for the temporal collisions of the present in which techno-culture sits side-by-side with the marketing of retro; new factory labour is supplemented by the re-emergence of nineteenth-century workhouses and home-based cottage industries; walled suburban enclaves are policed by private militias like feudal estates; and a modern police-force (nominally subject to public scrutiny) is replaced by hired guards working for a nouveau riche appropriately called the 'gentry'. Throughout their economic analysis, nothing of this residual character is hinted at, although it profoundly stamps the economic reality they seek to explain.

Philosophically, the new Italians' consolidation of a selective past is an intellectual failure they are powerless to avoid; but it is, at the same time, a deliberate strategy: it is this convenient combination we have to grasp, in fact, if we are to understand the book's interstitial logic. Caught in the traditions floundering in Hegel's wake, outmaneuvered by his system, and left with little more than the Nietzschean option of aestheticizing thought in the micro-rebellions of the will to truth, the new Italians are forced to go back to those who preceded Hegel (while, of course, silently drawing on Hegel at every step). To find a way out of Hegel's thinking they do not so much defeat him on the terrain of theory as transport themselves to a past that did not know him. Spinoza, or rather 'Spinoza', the 'first communist before Marx' of their creation, plays this role of anachronistic authority as *the* philosopher of modernity.

At the end of the day, though, one cannot really evaluate the book on the basis of refutations or plaudits of individual arguments and assumptions alone. For it is not just this or that observation that should be placed in question, but the book's entire apparatus of seeing and presenting. An adequate response to the book, in other words, demands a counter-narrative because what is at issue is not simply a book but the '68ist amalgam it represents. To marshal such a narrative requires more ground-clearing than I am at liberty to elaborate here, but it might be useful to mark the lineaments of such an effort. First, it necessitates having to understand the relationship of the anti-dialectical Nietzschean tradition to political anarchism as such.[51] In turn, this should prompt an inquiry into the demonization of the always criminal 'State' in contemporary cultural theory – a State that is usually posed as an ontological category rather than a locally varied, or contradictory structure – leading to immense confusion between left and right variants of anti-capitalist positions.[52]

Empire's return mounts a conception of history as a shop window filled with texts of glossy revolutionary allure. Hardt and Negri's gestures towards revolutionary workers is vital to understand, because it marks the pathology of the paralytic moment.[53]

Their writing takes the form of a conceit that has very little to do with workers, but rather the excited 'quotation' of workers' recorded activities in pursuit of a transportable inner spirit wrung from this history of others' making. Dissident youth, sick and tired of the world, latch on to the discourse of the workers' movement with the sincere desire of effecting finally, and forever, what the workers' movement itself failed to achieve: the end of commodity fetishism and the alienation of labour. But *Empire* has an auteurist or culinary devotion to the events of these histories, and as such they are no longer histories but prophecies of a coming millenarian return of the 'multitude' – a term redolent of the New Testament.

But the term 'multitude' betrays a reverse teleology that is religious in form: their designated 'multitudo fidelium'.[54, 55] Negri's political and intellectual formation in 1950s Catholic radicalism in Italy may be worth some mention in this context, although it has received almost no commentary. Most reviewers of the book have had very little to say about Negri's early inspirations in Catholic radicalism – not entirely unrelated to the universal harmony of his later vision. As an activist in l'Intesa, the organization of Catholic Universities in the 1950s, Negri had been 'assiduous on points of doctrine' and 'a fervent organizer of 'manifestations in honor of St. Anthony' and a dedicated student of St. Thomas.'[56] If it is unfair to reduce Negri's choices to symptoms of his Catholic training, it is no less problematic to pretend they have no bearing on *Empire*'s methodology or on its philosophical grounding in a 'materialist' theology. It should prompt interest, certainly, that a book which sees fit to dub the brilliant human rights advocate and internationalist theorist, Richard Falk, an 'idealist' and 'reformist' found solace in a veiled theology.[57] The millenarian tinge of this new 'materialism' of Negri's is only one of the familiar paradoxes of anarchism. For the all or nothing of non-compliance typically resolves itself into the normality of power simply because the all is always too much.

Back in the early 1960s, Tronti's principal thesis had been that 'the American workers are the hidden face of the international working class' and that 'today's U.S. is the theoretical problem for the future of us all.'[58] The new Italians seem now to have literally adopted his ardent faith that the United States would eventually show Europe the 'never-yet-seen techniques of political

use of the capitalist economic machine by the working class.' The
ultimate problem is that Hardt and Negri, against all expectations,
fail to see the ambiguity in these words, equating Tronti's 'working class' with the 'multitude' of a theoretical Americana.[59] The
new sovereignty is indeed, as Hardt and Negri say, that very
'indeterminacy, movement, creativity, ambiguity' of globalization.[60] But perhaps they forget that, just for this reason, the
dream-like desire for fluid social boundaries blurs the crude
imperialism of American *realpolitik*. The enemy of revolution in
the neo-liberal age is not 'the State,' but the sovereign, freely
experimenting, hybrid subjects of corporate utopia against whom
the state (or one version of it, at any rate) continues to be the last
refuge. The left fights in *that* space, or it refuses to fight.

Notes

1. Raymond Williams, 'Beyond Actually Existing Socialism', *Problems in Materialism and Culture*, London, New York: Verso 1980, pp. 252–3.
2. Michael Hardt and Antonio Negri, *Empire*, Cambridge, MA and London: Harvard University Press 2000, p. 66.
3. In addition to the coverage in the *New York Times* and Charlie Rose – neither of which has been known to have much truck with long books of theory that tirelessly quote Polybius and Rosa Luxemburg – see the coverage, for example, in Michael Elliott, 'The Wrong Side of the Barricades,' *Time Magazine*, July 23, 2001, p. 39. Elliott interestingly avers that Hardt and Negri are really on to something, provided they lost the Marx, who only gets in their way.
4. It seems odd, in retrospect, that the definitive experimentalist political text of the generation of 1968 was not Oskar Negt and Alexander Kluge's *Public Sphere and Experience*, which seemed perfectly suited for the task, but Deleuze and Guattari's *Capitalism and Schizophrenia*. The former sought a bridging rhetoric, combining some serious homework with novel and ener-getic institutional analyses of the media, labour, and the changes worked upon the latter by the former in the forging of new constituencies. It appears the natural predecessor to a work of *Empire's* ambitions. But the authors are drawn instead to the self-consciously prophetic work of schizoanalysis and its post-Freudian rampage against the bourgeois liberation of mere subjectivity.
5. See *Empire*, p. 62 on Deleuze and Guattari's 'apparatus of capture'.
6. For example, *Theory, Culture and Society* vol. 7, pp. 2–3, Special Issue on 'Global Culture', Mike Featherstone, ed., (June 1990); Anthony King, ed., *Culture, Globalization and the World System: Contemporary Conditions for the Repre-sentation of Identity* (1991); David Yergin and Joseph Stanislaw, *The Commanding Heights: The Battle Between Government and the Marketplace That Is Remaking the Modern World* (1998); David Held, *Democracy and the Global Order: From the Modern State to Cosmopolitan Governance* (1995).

7. Anthony Giddens, *Modernity and Self-Identity*, Stanford: Stanford University Press 1991, p. 9.

8. This is a standard view in international relations circles (in the work, for example, of Rosenau and Gilpin), but also (and more surprisingly) in left social studies. Benjamin Lee, for example, inexplicably considers the United States (as opposed to China) a 'weak-state' society. See 'Critical Internationalism,' *Public Culture*, vol. 7, no. 3 (Spring 1995), p. 581. But does he not, then, concur with Deleuze and Guattari's formulation on the *Urstaat* in *Anti-Oedipus?* 'It is beneath the blows of private property, then of commodity production, that the State witnesses its decline' (p. 218). Capitalism is here cast as a saviour: it saves us from the excesses of (in Deleuze and Guattari's words) the fearful 'Asiatic state'.

9. For a fuller discussion of council communism and related interwar tendencies, see Paul Mattick, *Anti-Bolshevik Communism*, London: Merlin Press, 1978. Note especially pages 83–5.

10. The constellation, as I am using it here, roughly coincides with the contributors to Paolo Virno and Michael Hardt, eds., *Radical Thought in Italy: A Potential Politics*, Minneapolis: University of Minnesota Press 1996. Agamben, however (who plays a large role in this anthology) is not 'new Italian' on the terms I have laid out here since he does not trace his formation to the *autonomia* movements. Nevertheless, both Negri and Agamben base their political assessments on the idea that the exception is the rule, and that 'naked life' is not only *in* politics, but coincident with the political realm, a realm of the 'productive *bios*.' Hardt and Negri spell out their differences with Agamben in *Empire*, pp. 366, 421.

11. Hardt, 'Introduction: Laboratory Italy', *Radical Thought in Italy*, p. 1.

12. For political background, see Mark Gilbert, 'Italy's Third Fall', *Journal of Modern Italian Studies* vol. 2 no. 2 (1997) pp. 221–31; Alexander Stille, 'Italy: The Convulsions of Normalcy', *New York Review of Books*, 6 June 1996, pp. 42–6; Rudi Ghedini, 'After the Fall of Bologna: The Decline of Italy's Red City', *Le Monde Diplomatique*, September 2000. The contemporary Italian situation is well presented in Vittorio Bufacchi and Simon Burgess, *Italy Since 1989*, London: Macmillan 1998.

13. 'New Times' is associated with circles around the (now defunct) British journal *Marxism Today* in the late 1980s and early 1990s. They argued that systemic transformations in capitalism had forced the left to place a new emphasis on consumerism, abandon the emphasis on industrial labour, and jettison the goals of the welfare state. See Stuart Hall and Martin Jacques, eds., *New Times: The Changing Face of Politics in the 1990s*, London, New York: Verso 1990.

14. It is beyond the scope of this essay to provide a critique of post-Fordist conceits, but readers may want to consult the following concise accounts of the problems found in them: Neil Lazarus 'Doubting the New World Order: Marxism and Postmodernist Social Theory', *differences*, vol. 3, no. 3 (1991), pp. 94–138; Alex Callinicos, *Against Postmodernism: A Marxist Critique*, Oxford: Polity Press 1990; and Daniel T. McGee, 'Post-Marxism: The Opiate of the Intellectuals', *Modern Language Quarterly*, vol. 58, no. 2 (June 1997), pp. 201–25.

15. According to Varcellone, the phrase animated the entire movement throughout the 1970s, and functions now in the present as a structure of

feeling *(Radical Thought in Italy*, p. 2); for 'the will to be against', see *Empire*, 204, 274.

16. Mario Tronti, *Operai e capitale*, Torino: Einaudi 1977.

17. Mario Tronti, 'The Strategy of Refusal', *Semiotexte*, vol. 3, no. 3 (1980), p. 30.

18. See Virno, 'The Ambivalence of Disenchantment' (RTI, 20, 26, 28).

19. Robert Reich, *The Work of Nations*, New York: Alfred A. Knopf, 1991; Anthony Giddens, 'The Contours of High Modernity,' in *Modernity and Self-Identity: Self and Society in the Late Modern Age*, Stanford: Stanford UP, 1991, 10–34.

20. *Empire*, p. 290.

21. *Radical Thought in Italy*, p. 132.

22. Ibid., p. 22.

23. *Empire*, pp. 61, 64.

24. *Radical Thought in Italy*, p. 135.

25. Antonio Negri, 'Twenty Theses on Marx: Interpretation of the Class Situation Today,' in Saree Makdisi, Cesare Casarino, Rebecca E. Karl, *Marxism Beyond Marxism*, New York, London: Routledge, 1996, 165, 172, 175.

26. *Radical Thought in Italy*, p. 142.

27. *Empire*, p. 61.

28. Tom Brass, 'A-Way with Their Wor(l)d: Rural Labourers through the Postmodern Prism,' *Economic & Political Weekly*, vol. 28, no. 23 (1993), pp. 1162–8 traces the conservative heritage of the popular culture *as* resistance thesis that dominates Hardt and Negri's 'revolution of the already is': 'An almost identical concept of non-confrontation with the state, a form of indirect political action known as the "theory of small deeds," was actually pioneered by Russian populists during the late 19th century [Utechin 1964]. More importantly, much of the theory which prefigures the "resistance" framework is already present in an earlier text by James Scott [1968: 94ff, 119ff] where he endorses both the "limited good" argument of George Foster [1965] and the "culture of poverty" thesis advanced by Oscar Lewis [1962],' p. 1163.

29. *Empire*, pp. xv, 25.

30. 'The globalization of markets, far from being simply the horrible fruit of capitalist entrepreneurship, was actually the result of the desires and demands of Taylorist, Fordist, and disciplined labor power across the world.' (Ibid., p. 266.)

31. Ibid., p. 43.

32. Richard Falk & Andrew Strauss, 'On the Creation of a Global Peoples Assembly: Legitimacy and Power of Popular Sovereignty', *Stanford Journal of International Law*, vol. 36, no. 2 (2000), pp. 191–219; and 'Toward a Global Parliament', *Foreign Affairs*, January/February 2001, pp. 212–20.

33. *Empire*, p. 50.

34. Whatever critique one might offer of the political legacies of the Russian revolution, anti-Bolshevik Marxism typically, and by an inexorable logic, ends by 'discovering' the beauty of the United States, which is then weirdly taken to have realized socialism's original aims in spite of its annihilation of actual socialists. C. L. R. James, to take only one example, seriously argued in the 1950s that American popular culture perfectly recorded working class interests, and witnessed a flawless correspondence between the

popular will and a government forced to do its bidding: the people had come
to power!

35. *Empire*, p. 223.

36. Ibid., p. 357.

37. Saskia Sassen, *Globalization and its Discontents*, New York: The New Press
1998, p. xxix; and *The Global City: New York, London, Tokyo*, Princeton: Princeton University Press 1991, pp. 3–34. *Empire* takes its discussion of 'non-places'
from Marc Augé.

38. Hardt and Negri's recent op. ed. in the *New York Times* offered a
startling illustration of ambivalence in cultural theory, in this case self-serving.
Written to explain what the anti-globalization protesters at the Genoa summit
really wanted, the authors concluded – in spite of the protesters' emphatic
declarations to the contrary – that the Genovese rebels were not against
globalization. In what must have come as great relief to the editors of the
Times, the authors further argued that the insurgents did not see the United
States as the major antagonist in the new global order (which also contradicts
the protesters' reported statements). The prominence of the forum in the
Times undoubtedly moves readers to associate Hardt and Negri's work with
the rebelling forces, as though proof of their prophetic and radical aims.
Actually, the analysis indicates their forcing of the movement into the theses
of *Empire*. Michael Hardt and Antonio Negri, 'What the Protesters in Genoa
Want', *New York Times*, 20 July 2001, p. A23.

39. *Empire*, p. 223.

40. Ibid., p. 294.

41. Political organization itself, in their words, should be seen as a kind of
'Exodus'. Because new Italian thinkers have found success primarily abroad
in the American theoretical establishment (that is, in a kind of exodus), the
theorist's person is analogized in the nomadism of labour, which is cast as a
restless 'refusal and search for liberation' – rather than the typically coercive
migration of workers to harvests or factory towns fleeing landlords or a callous
police-force (*Empire*, pp. 234–5, 212–13).

42. *Empire*, p. 34.

43. Ibid., p. xvi and passim.

44. Theodor Adorno, *Beethoven: The Philosophy of Music*, Stanford: Stanford
University Press 1998, p. 141.

45. Warren Montag has shown that Spinoza tends to tell us three stories
at once: 'the story of God, the story of Nature and the story of God-as-Nature,
or, the story of transcendence, the story of immanence and the story of
transcendence as immanence'. Warren Montag, *Bodies, Masses, Power: Spinoza
and His Contemporaries*, London and New York: Verso 1999, p. 4 as quoted in
John Kraniauskas, 'Empire or multitudes: Transnational Negri', *Radical Philosophy*, vol. 103 no. 35, September/October 2000, p. 36.

46. Howard P. Kainz, *An Introduction to Hegel: The Stages of Modern Philosophy*, Athens: Ohio University Press 1996, p. 21.

47. For example, in Thomas Dumm, interview with Michael Hardt, 'Sovereignty, Multitudes, Absolute Democracy', *Theory and Event*, http://
muse.jhu.edu/journals/theory_&_event/v004/4.3hardt.html, p. 6.

48. *Empire*, p. xvi.

49. As Jurgen Habermas was pointing out long before the Schmitt revival
took shape in the English-speaking world, Schmitt plays a curious role in

current cultural theory. His approach to the political is about freeing political actors from ethical constraints in the practice of sovereign power. He plays a compensatory role here, saying what the authors are unwilling to enact – that is, striking the note absent from their discourse. His conservative credentials bring his views more in accord with the conservatism that attends the neo-liberal age to which the new Italians form an adversarial adjunct. And yet, since Schmitt was radical in his earlier period, he has been cleansed by the decades into a new acceptability – a conformism which is not a conformism. See Habermas, 'The Horrors of Autonomy: Carl Schmitt in English', *The New Conservatism: Cultural Criticism and the Historians' Debate*, Cambridge, MA: MIT Press 1989, pp. 128–39.

    50. *A Thousand Plateaus*, p. 23.

    51. As Holmes points out in *Integral Europe*, the Sorelians 'emphasized the potential of a cultural assemblage to serve as the basis of collectivity . . . . They sought to formulate a politics that could . . . engage directly the human substance of an integral lifeworld.' Nicola Badaloni has also shown how Sorel is key to understanding the interwar period from which many of the new Italian ideas are drawn, including its ambiguous political location. A theory that abandoned 'the theme of the necessity of socialism and its replacement by a combinatory of various possibilities, connects with the co-penetration of the juridical and the economic. He presented this result (in a way which does not differ from that which, fifty years later, the structuralist school of French Marxism was to arrive at) as the authentic thought of Marx.' Results are achieved 'in spite of man's intellectual consciousness'. See Chantal Mouffe, *Gramsci and Marxist Theory* London, Boston: Routledge & Kegan Paul 1979, p. 82.

    52. And nowhere more emphatically than in *Anti-Oedipus*, where Deleuze and Guattari write: '*there has never been but a single State*, the State-as-dog that "speaks with flaming roars" ' (the latter part of their statement is a quote from Nietzsche) (p. 192). In response to that singular evil, on the very next page, they posit 'the dream of a spiritual empire, wherever temporal empires fall into decadence' (p. 193).

    53. One illustration of this element in Negri's work can be found in *The Labor of Dionysus*, p. 28–9.

    54. *Empire*, p. 429.

    55. Throughout the *Prison Notebooks*, Gramsci describes the scholastic national-cultural training of Italian high intellectuals and the Catholic excrescences on modern thought that had remained resilient in the face of modernization. It is ironic that the new Italian amalgam – in particular, Negri whose status as a prisoner gives him a superficial resemblance to Gramsci in the minds of younger theorists – would gain from association with Gramsci's prior fame. One could say – above all in their Sorelian echoes – that they were the cult he sought to expose. See, the entries on Sorel in Antonio Gramsci, *Prison Notebooks*, Vol. II, 58, 98, 112, 123, 139–41, 168–72, 193–4, 235.

    56. Drake, *The Revolutionary Mystique and Terrorism in Contemporary Italy*, p. 52.

    57. *Empire*, p. 417.

    58. Tronti, 'Workers and Capital', *Telos*, vol. 14 (Winter 1972), pp. 40, 62.

    59. Tronti, 'Workers and Capital', p. 62.

    60. *Empire*, p. 39.

Toni Negri in Perspective

Alex Callinicos

If there were any doubt that the anti-capitalist movement represents a major revival of the left on a world scale, it was removed
by the vast demonstration against the G8 summit in Genoa on 21
July 2001.[1] Around 30,000 people, the overwhelming majority of
them from Italy itself, took part in the protest, despite the
extreme violence displayed by the police. The youth, confidence
and militancy of the demonstrators offered clear evidence that
the Italian left – after nearly a quarter of a century of defeat and
demoralization – was in the process of being renewed.

This kind of revival is, however, a complex affair. It is easy enough
to think that a new left necessarily bases itself on new ideas. The
rhetoric of some of the leading figures in the anti-capitalist movement often expresses this thought. The stress that Naomi Klein,
for example, lays on 'the decentralised, non-hierarchical structure
of the movement' and its 'web-like structure' is intended to highlight the novelty of the contemporary movement against corporate
globalization.[2] But new struggles always involve elements of continuity as well as discontinuity with the past. Bodies of thought
formulated in different conditions, and marginalized in the recent
past, can re-emerge to exert a major influence in a new movement.

The ideas of *Empire* are having a practical effect. One of the
main currents in the anti-capitalist movement is autonomism.
This has two main political characteristics: (1) the rejection of the
Leninist conception of organization; and (2) the adoption of
substitutionist forms of action in which a politically enlightened
elite acts on behalf of the masses. Autonomism is in fact a diverse

political formation. The most notorious version is represented by the anarchist Black Bloc, whose pursuit of violent confrontation with the state played into the police's hands at Genoa. More attractive is the Italian autonomist coalition *Ya Basta!*, which combines an uncompromising rejection of the political establishment – including the parties of the reformist left – with, on the one hand, the adoption of imaginative forms of non-violent direct action and, on the other, contesting municipal elections, sometimes successfully. *Ya Basta!*, which itself acts as an umbrella for different views and emphases, overlaps with the *Tute Bianche*, known after the white overalls they used to wear on demonstrations, most famously at the Prague S26 protests in September 2000. Naomi Klein calls the social centres that tend to provide *Ya Basta!* with its main base of activity 'windows – not only into another way to live, disengaged from the state, but also into a new politics of engagement'.[3] The *Tute Bianche*'s statements are impregnated with the language of *Empire*. Thus their best known leader, Luca Casarini, said after Genoa:

> We have talked of Empire, or better of an imperial logic in the government of the world. This means the erosion of national sovereignty. Not the end, but an erosion and its redefinition in a global, imperial, framework. In Genoa we saw this at work, with the scenarios of war this implies. On how to oppose this imperial logic we have all still been unprepared.[4]

Such evidence of *Empire*'s political influence should come as no surprise. For Toni Negri is the foremost philosopher of Italian autonomism. Born in 1936, he has recently completed the remainder of a sentence in Italy for his alleged part in the Red Brigades' campaign of armed terror during the late 1970s. His plight is an indication of the specific historical context in which autonomism first took shape, during the profound crisis that Italian society experienced during the 1970s. Any assessment of *Empire* therefore presupposes an understanding of that context, and of the development of Negri's thought.

The Italian earthquake and the rise of autonomism

With the important exception of the Portuguese Revolution, the great upturn in workers' struggles that swept through Western

Europe during the late 1960s and the first half of the 1970s reached its high point in Italy.[5] The student revolt of 1967–68 and the explosion of strikes in the 'Hot Autumn' of 1969 marked the prelude to a massive wave of workers' struggles that fed into a broader social radicalization expressed, for example, in the defeat of the ruling Christian Democratic (DC) oligarchy in the 1974 referendum on divorce This was a climate that favoured the emergence in the late 1960s of a substantial far left dominated by three main organizations – *Avanguardia Operaia, Lotta Continua* and PDUP (Party of Proletarian Unity for Communism). The far left exerted significant influence in the most militant sections of the working class. In the mid-1970s they could mobilize 20,000–30,000 people in Milan alone. By this time, however, Italy was caught up in a massive economic, social and political crisis. In Washington and Bonn the country was perceived as the sick man of Western capitalism. The corrupt and authoritarian DC regime was manifestly in a state of advanced decay. In the regional and local elections of June 1975 the left won 47 percent of the vote, while the DC's share fell to 35 percent. But within five years the Italian workers' movement had suffered a series of shattering defeats from which it is only now beginning to recover.

Two main factors were responsible for this disaster.[6] First, and more important, the Italian Communist Party (PCI) came to the rescue of the DC. Tobias Abse writes, 'For all its resistance to the worker and student rebelliousness of 1967–69, and its equivoca- tion over the divorce referendum of 1974, the PCI paradoxically profited from both as an electoral force'.[7] In parallel, the PCI- dominated trade union confederation CGIL absorbed much of the shopfloor militancy that had exploded in the late 1960s – for example, by establishing factory councils.[8] The restoration of PCI control was helped by the way in which, as unemployment began to rise in the mid-1970s, workplace struggles became much more fragmented and defensive than they had been during the Hot Autumn.

In the June 1976 parliamentary elections the PCI's share of the vote peaked at 34.4 percent. But PCI leader Enrico Berlinguer responded by helping to bale Italian capitalism out. After the Chilean coup of September 1973 he offered the DC a 'historic compromise'. Though the PCI was blocked from actually taking office thanks to US intervention, in 1976–79 the party gave its backing to a series of 'Governments of National Solidarity' headed by ultra-Machiavellian DC politician and ally of the Vatican Giulio Andreotti. The PCI used its dominance of the workers' movement to overcome resistance to the government's programme of austerity measures, thereby helping to stablilize Italian capitalism.

A secondary factor in the crisis was the weakness of the revolutionary left. The dominant version of Marxism on the Italian far left in the 1960s was Maoism. The idea that peasant guerrillas had overthrown capitalism in China opened the door to a belief that there were short cuts to revolution that could avoid the lengthy and difficult task of winning the support of the majority of the working class. In the climate of intense radicalization in the late 1960s this had taken the form of building factory base committees (CUBs) outside the unions.

By the mid-1970s the three main far left organizations swung sharply to the right, developing a strategy based on the assumption that the 1976 elections would lead to a left government in which the far left might participate, and which would carry through a far-ranging programme of reforms. In the event, the DC vote actually rose, the revolutionary left only won 1.5 percent of the vote, and the PCI formed a coalition with the right rather than with the rest of the left. The result was the descent of *Avanguardia*, *Lotta Continua* and PDUP into crisis, and the astonishingly rapid disintegration of their organizations.[9]

This was not, however, the end of mass struggle. Early 1977 saw the development of a new student movement that rapidly spread to unemployed youth, in which *Autonomia Operaia*, a loose federation of revolutionary collectives, exerted a growing influence. It began when students occupied Rome University in February 1977. Paul Ginsborg writes:

> *Autonomia Operaia*, much to the disgust of the feminists, controlled the occupation and limited freedom of speech. On 19 February Luciano Lama, head of the CGIL, heavily protected by trade union and PCI stewards, came to address the occupation . . . In a tragic scene of mutual incomprehension, Lama was shouted down, and violent clashes broke out between the autonomi and the stewards of the PCI. A fortnight later a demonstration of some 60,000 young people in the capital degenerated into a four-hour guerrilla battle with police. Shots were fired on both sides, and a part of the demonstrators chanted a macabre slogan in praise of the P38 pistol, the chosen weapon of the autonomi.[10]

The movement spread rapidly, with a series of violent confrontations with the forces of the state in which two young activists, Francesco Lorusso and Georgina Masi, were shot dead by the carabinieri in Bologna and Rome respectively.[11] As Abse puts it:

> The original student unrest of early 1977 was a confused but authentic expression of the alienation and despair of large masses of Italian youth, a protest against the climate of economic crisis and political conformism that marked the regime of national solidarity. Its initial expression anticipated many elements of later British punk culture – a penchant for the deliberately but harmlessly bizarre that took the form of fantasmatic identification with 'Indians' (American rather than subcontinental).[12]

For all its attractive qualities, however, and the anger it expressed, the movement of 1977, developing as it did in the context of rising mass unemployment especially among young people, was inherently liable to come into conflict with the organized working class. This liability became reality as a result of the political influence of autonomism. *Autonomia Operaia*, which first emerged in March 1973, was an internally heterogeneous formation on which Negri's writings exerted a particularly important influence.[13] His intellectual background lay in *operaismo* – 'workerism' – a distinctively Italian Marxist theoretical current whose most important figure was Mario Tronti. The focus of this Marxism was on the direct conflict between capital and labour in the immediate process of production. Tronti explored the interplay between capitalist and proletarian strategies. Thus he saw the Keynesian welfare state devleloped in the US under the New Deal as a response to, and an attempt to incorporate, the 'mass worker' forged during the second industrial revolution of the late nineteenth and early twentieth centuries.[14]

Operaismo was merely one of a number of Marxist theoretical currents that came to focus during the 1960s and 1970s on what they call the capitalist labour process – the German 'capital-logic' school is another example. This preoccupation made sense at a time of intense industrial conflict in which strong workplace organization defied bosses and trade union officials alike. In 1974 Negri could still write that the factory was 'the privileged site of both the refusal of labour and the attack upon the rate of profit'.[15] But in the late 1970s, as rank and file militancy crumbled in the face of economic crisis and the historic compromise, he preserved the theoretical categories of *operaismo* while, as Abse puts it, he turned it 'into virtually the opposite of its former ideological self'.[16] His key theoretical move was to replace the concept of the 'mass worker' with that of the 'social worker'.

Negri argued that the process of capitalist exploitation now took place on a society-wide scale, and that consequently socially and economically marginalized groups such as students, the unemployed and casual labourers must be counted as core sections of the proletariat. Indeed, relative to these groups, the old 'mass workers' in the big factories of northern Italy appeared like a privileged labour aristocracy. According to the following passage, merely receiving a wage made a worker an exploiter on a par with management:

> Some groups of workers, some sections of the working class, remain tied to the dimension of the wage, to its mystified terms. In other words, they are living off income as revenue. Inasmuch, they are stealing and expropriating proletarian surplus-value – they are participating in the social labour racket – on the same terms as their management. These positions – and the trade union practice that fosters them – are to be fought, with violence if necessary. It will not be the first time that a march of the unemployed has entered a large factory so that they can destroy the arrogance of salaried income![17]

This kind of sophistry was more than theoretical nonsense. It offered an apparently 'Marxist' legitimation for the violent clashes that were developing between the autonomists and trade unionsts.[18] The incitement to attack employed workers was part of a more general cult of violence. Negri wrote:

> Proletarian violence, in so far as it is a positive allusion to communism, is an essential element of the dynamic of communism. To suppress the violence of this process can only deliver it – tied hand and foot – to capital. Violence is a first, immediate, and vigorous affirmation of the necessity of communism. It does not provide the solution, but is fundamental.[19]

Meanwhile others were taking this cult of violence to its logical conclusion. The Red Brigades (BR) were formed in the early 1970s, but it was in the climate of violence and despair of 1977–78 that they were encouraged to escalate their campaign of armed terror against the Italian state. The BR's most spectacular act was the kidnapping and murder of the DC leader and former prime minister Aldo Moro in the spring of 1978. The BR didn't just target state officials, but also trade unionists whom they regarded as collaborating with the state. These tactics were given some spurious legitimacy by the strong support the PCI gave to governmental measures that drastically restricted civil liberties. But the effect was to isolate the entire far left, and to unleash a wave of severe repression that destroyed the BR and swept many others into prison.

Faced with a divided and weakened left, and benefiting from the PCI's complicity, the employers went onto the offensive. In October 1979 Fiat succeeded in sacking 61 militants at its Mirafiori plant in Turin, accusing them of having been involved in violence. The following September it announced a plan to sack 14,000 workers in the most militant sections. Even the PCI leadership recognized that this attack would weaken them along with the rest of the workers' movement. Berlinguer went to the factory gates and declared his support for an occupation. But he had served his purpose. Exploiting divisions in the Turin workplace, Fiat won a crushing victory. A total of 23,000 workers, many of them militants, were sacked. Comparing the conflict to the great British miners' strike of 1984–85, Abse writes, 'Fiat's real aim was to alter the whole balance of power in the factory, and to reassert a control over the labour force and the production process it had lost in 1969'.[20] Its success in achieving this objective set the stage for the resurgence of Italian capitalism in the 1980s whose greatest symbol would be the rise of Silvio Berlusconi.

Negri rewrites Marx as Foucault

Negri was one of the casualties of this defeat. He was arrested in Padua in April 1979 on trumped-up charges of master-minding the Red Brigades and Moro's kidnapping. Held without trial for four years, he was only freed in 1983 after having been elected to parliament as a deputy for the libertarian Radical Party, and then fled into exile in France. His jail sentence was handed out *in absentia* in 1984.[21] That same year *Marx Beyond Marx*, perhaps Negri's most important book, appeared in English. Based on seminars that Negri had given at Louis Althusser's invitation at the *École Normale Supérieure* in Paris in 1978, it was written at precisely the moment of disaster for the Italian left.

The editor of the English edition of *Marx Beyond Marx* called it 'one of the most crucial documents in European Marxism since ... well, since maybe never'.[22] This enthusiastic description at least captures the ambition of the book. For what Negri in efect seeks to do is narrow Marxism down from a comprehensive theory of the driving forces of historical change to a mere theory of power. He does so on the basis of a reading of the *Grundrisse* – the text, written in 1857–58, that represents the first in the succession of huge manuscripts culminating in the first volume of *Capital* a decade later.

Negri, however, regards *Capital* as a flawed work that 'served to reduce critique to economic theory, to annihilate subjectivity in objectivity, to subject the subversive capacity of the proletariat to the reorganising and repressive intelligence of capitalist power'. 'Subjectivity' is the key word here. For Negri, history is 'reduced to collective relations of force', the clash between rival class subjectivities – capital and labour: 'The *Grundrisse* aims at a theory of the subjectivity of the working class against the profitable theory of capitalist subjectivity'.[23]

Negri's transformation of labour into a kind of absolute subject is reflected in his theory of crisis. He argues that 'the law of fall of the profit rate derives from the fact that *necessary labour is a rigid quantity*' – that is, when capitalists seek to reduce the share of necessary labour (required to reproduce labour power) in the working day and thereby to drive up the rate of exploitation, they encounter 'a force less and less willing to be subjected, less and less available to compression'. This obdurate resistance signifies '*the autonomy of the working class from the development of capital*'.[24]

Now Marx isn't God. There is nothing sacred about his theories, and therefore there is no crime in revising them. The interesting questions concern the direction of Negri's revisions and whether or not they allow us more effectively to engage with the contemporary world. Critically Negri seeks to transform Marxism into a theory of power. Thus he argues that 'the capitalist relation is immediately a relation of power'. He attaches special importance to the fact that the *Grundrisse* begins with a lengthy discussion of money. Here Marx moves '*from the critique of money to the critique of power*'.[25]

Or it might be better to say that by focusing on money Marx directly engages with capital as a form of power. The development of money under capitalism, which reaches its climax in the credit system (what these days are called the fundamental markets), represents in a highly distorted and antagonistic form the socialization of production. In starting with money in the *Grundrisse*, Marx operates with 'a tendential scheme of *social capital*'. He is thus able to anticipate the subsequent development of capitalism as 'a form of production which becomes increasingly more social, in which the modern function of value is transformed into a function of command, of domination, and of intervention on the social fractions of necessary labour and accumulation. The state is here the 'synthesis of civil society'.²⁶

Thus, according to Negri, Marx in the *Grundrisse*, anticipates the emergence of the Keynesian welfare state:

> Marx indicated, and often too frequently, especially in the *Grundrisse*, that to say state is only another way of saying capital. The development of the mode of production leads us to recognise that to say state is the *only* way to say capital: a socialised capital, a capital whose accumulation is done in terms of power, a transformation of the theory of command; the launching into circuit and the development of the state of the multinationals.²⁷

Here Negri rejoins the classical preoccupation of *operaismo* with the strategies pursued by the 'collective capitalist', increasingly through the state, to contain and dominate the 'mass worker' of Fordist assembly line production. But Negri gives a radically different spin to this analysis by replacing the 'mass worker' with the 'social worker':

> The capitalist supersession of the form of value – what Marx calls the process of real subsumption – dislocates the relations of production as a whole. It transforms exploitation into a global social relation. Jail equals factory … In reality, the operation of real subsumption does not eliminate the [class] antagonism, but rather displaces it to the social level. Class struggle does not disappear; it is rather transformed into all the moments of everyday life. The daily life of a proletarian is posited as a whole against the domination of capital.²⁸

The class struggle is everywhere, therefore, and so too is the proletariat. Whoever experiences the domination of capital is part of the working class. The logic of the class struggle within the process of production itself implies the 'refusal of work' – workers rebelling against wage relation itself. This is implicitly communist because communism is nothing but 'the abolition of work'. In asserting themselves within the productive process, workers carve out a space under their own control. They become, as Negri puts it, 'self valorising', breaking the connection between wage labour and the realization of their needs. The confrontation between this refusal of work and 'social capital' is increasingly reduced to a relationship of force; 'Once capital and global labour power have completely become social classes – each independent and capable of self valorising activity – then the law of value can only represent the power (*potenza*) and violence of the relationship. It is the synthesis of the relations of force'.[29]

This increasingly violent confrontation takes place everywhere: 'The struggle against the capitalist organisation of production, of the job market, of the working day, of the restructuring of energy, of family life, etc, etc, all this involves the people, the community, the choice of lifestyle. To be communist today means *to live as* a communist'.[30] Thus, paradoxically, a form of Marxism that was originally obsessed with the struggle at the point of production flips over into its opposite, something much closer to the post-Marxist obsession with a plurality of power relations and social movements.

Indeed, Negri explicitly connects his version of Marxism with poststructuralism, declaring, 'The theory of surplus value breaks down the [class] antagonism into a microphysics of power'.[31] It was Michel Foucault who in a series of key texts in the mid-1970s developed a critique of Marxism based on the idea that domination consists in a plurality of power relations that cannot be removed by means of some comprehensive social transformation (this would, as in Stalinist Russia, merely reinstate a new apparatus of domination) but only resisted on a decentralized and localized basis.[32] What Negri does here is to take over Foucault's disintegration of the social totality into a multiplicity of micro-practices and claim that this is what Marx himself does, at least in the *Grundrisse*.

These allusions to Foucault are indicative of the extent to which Negri transforms historical materialism into a theory of power and subjectivity. This theory enabled him to observe the increasingly disastrous course taken by the class struggle in Italy in the late 1970s with serene indifference. Thus he wrote in 1977:

The balance of power has been reversed . . . the working class, its sabotage, are the stronger power – above all, the only source of relationality and value. From now on it becomes impossible, even in theory, to forget this paradox produced by the struggles: the more the form of domination perfects itself, the more empty it becomes; the more the working class resists, the more it is full of rationality and value . . . We are here, we are uncrushable, and we are in the majority.[33]

One can, if one likes, find something magnificent in this defiant optimism. But if Marxist theory is to offer political guidance and responsible leadership, then it has to strive accurately to plot the oscillations of the class struggle. At much the same time, Tony Cliff was developing his analysis of the shift in the balance of class forces in capital's favour in Britain.[34] Cliff's appreciation of the situation of course proved much more accurate than Negri's. In Italy also, Negri's refusal to face facts came under sharp attack at the time even from within the autonomist movement – for example, by Sergio Bologna:

There have been many small (or big) battles, but in their course the political composition of the class has changed substantially in the factories, and certainly not in the direction indicated by Negri . . . In sum there has been a reassertion of reformist hegemony over the factories, one that is brutal and relentless in its efforts to dismember the class left and expel it from the factory.[35]

Bologna accused Negri of inventing 'a different social figure with which to impute the process of liberation from exploitation', of simply evading the real process of defeat the Italian working class was experiencing. These misjudgements were indeed symptoms of a deeper theoretical flaw. Negri is an admirer of the great early modern philosopher Spinoza, and wrote an important book about him, *The Savage Anomaly*, when he was first in prison at the end of the 1970s. Spinoza was very critical of explanations that treat what happens as the result of an assertion of will, whether the will in question was that of God or of humans. This way of proceeding was, Spinoza said, 'to take refuge in . . . the sanctuary of ignorance'.[36] But precisely this criticism can be applied to Negri's rewriting of Marx. To reduce history to the clash of rival class wills – the 'collective capitalist' versus the 'social worker' – is to explain nothing. The nature and development of struggles can only be properly understood once their objective context is reconstructed.

Thus Marx integrates his account of the class struggle – both within the immediate production process and more broadly in society – into a theory of the capitalist mode of production as a totality. The clashes between rival classes are only comprehensible against the background of the broader tendencies of the mode of production. Negri attributes to capitalists no motivation other than an abstract urge to dominate. Marx by contrast conceptualizes the bourgeoisie as an internally divided class caught up in competitive struggles among themselves. This is the sphere of what Marx – in the *Grundrisse* (though Negri ignores these passages) – calls 'many capitals'. The tendency of the rate of profit to fall is not just a product of the conflict between labour and capital in the immediate production process, but also of this competitive struggle, which drives capitalists to invest in labour-saving equipment.[37]

Negri's voluntarist theory of crisis was superficially attractive in the 1970s, when the first major postwar slump developed against the background of rising workers' struggles. Even then, however, it offered a wholly inadequate explanation of the crisis, which reflected a *general* fall in the rate of profit irrespective of the level of struggle in the society concerned. West Germany and the US were just as much victims as Italy or Britain, even though the level of class struggle was much lower in the first two countries than it was in the second two.[38] In any case, Negri's theory can't explain the currently developing global recession, which comes at a time when working-class combativity is still comparatively low.

Moreover, Marx is clear that as long as capitalist relations of production remain in place, the capitalists retain the upper hand. They can, as they did in the late 1970s and the 1980s, use their control of the means of production to weaken workers by closing plants and laying people off. That is why it is not enough to rebel at the point of production – workers need a generalized political movement that can seize power at the level of society as a whole and expropriate capital.

To say all this is not to fall guilty of the charge of 'objectivism' that Negri constantly flings around. Marxism posits a dialectic of objectivity and subjectivity, not the reduction of one term to the other, whether it be subject to object, as in the Althusserian notion of history as 'a process without a subject', or object to subject, as in Negri's voluntaristic rewriting of Marxism. Social structures – crucially the forces and relations of production – impose limits to what human actors can achieve, but they also constitute the capacities that these actors use when seeking to remake their world.[39]

From constituent power to Empire

Marx Beyond Marx represented an impasse in Negri's thought, since it sought theoretically to articulate the guiding principles of a political movement that went down to crushing defeat at the end of the 1970s. In his writings of the 1980s and 1990s that culminate in *Empire*, Negri sought to resituate and to develop the themes of *Marx Beyond Marx*. Many of these texts are devoted to the history of modern political thought, and as such are of value in their own right. But they also serve to reconstruct Negri's system. A brief survey of this nature can only highlight some key points.

Already in *Marx Beyond Marx* Negri had stressed what he called 'the principle of constitution', by which he means the capacity of struggle creatively to produce a qualitatively new structure that itself becomes the object of new struggles leading to further transformation.[40] In his later writings Negri greatly develops this idea. He traces the development of the idea of 'constituent power' – the collective capacity underlying specific constitutional forms to make and remake social and political structures – from its origins in Renaissance humanism, through early modern political thought (crucially Machiavelli and Spinoza) to its increasingly clear articulation in the era of revolutions, culminating in Marx. Involved here is a conflict between two kinds of power – *potenza* versus *potere* (in French *puissance* versus *pouvoir*) – that is, the creative power of the masses (what Negri increasingly calls the 'multitude') versus the domination of capital.[41]

Negri offers a highly abstract conception of constituent power. It is 'a creative power [*puissance*] of being, in other words of concrete figures, of values, of institutions and orderings of the real. Constituent power [*pouvoir*] constitutes society in identifying the social and the political, in uniting them in a ontological bond.' According to Negri, Marx saw constituent power at work in capital in the way in which it violently created a new form of society in the era of primitive accumulation but also drew on the creative capacities of co-operation inherent in the multitude. Negri writes:

> Co-operation is in effect the living and productive pulsation of the *multitudo* . . . Co-operation is innovation and wealth, it is thus the basis of the creative surplus which defines the expression of the *multitudo*. It is on the abstraction, on the alienation and on the productive expropriation of the multitude that command is constructed.[42]

In Marx, the co-operative labour that is appropriated and exploited by capital is, of course, that of the working class. By reframing Marxist themes in a more abstract philosophical vocabulary, Negri is able to take advantage of their resonances (for example, the idea that capital is parasitic on the creative power of others) while sidelining any straightforward class analysis. But the same tendency to absolutize the subjectivity of the masses that we saw in Negri's writings of the 1970s is present here: 'All practice of constituent power, from its beginning to its end, in its origin as in its crisis, reveals the tension of the multitude tending to make itself the absolute subject of the processes of its power [*puissance*]'.[43]

Negri, however, goes beyond the subjectivism of his earlier writings when he poses the question of how 'a subject adequate to the absolute procedure' of constituent power is to be identified. The answer, he believes, is to be found in the writings of the 'second Foucault', in particular in his *History of Sexuality*: 'Man as Foucault describes him appears as a totality of resistances which deliver a capacity of absolute liberation, beyond all finalism that is not the expression of itself and of its reproduction. It is life that liberates itself in man, which opposes itself to everything that limits it and imprisons it'.[44]

The multitude when it strives to become the absolute subject of history is thus an expression of life. Negri thus seeks to ground his subjectivism in a form of vitalism – that is, in a metaphysical theory that sees the physical and social world in its entirety as expressions of some underlying life force. Negri is in fact indebted here less to Foucault, who is evasive if not confused when confronted with the philosophical implications of his theory of power, than to another key figure of French poststructuralism, Gilles

Deleuze.[45] Particularly in *Mille plateaux*, the second volume of his major theoretical collaboration with Félix Guattari, *Capitalisme et schizophrenie*, Deleuze conceives desire as an expression of life that, though constantly confined and stratified in historically specific constellations of power, equally constantly subverts and outflanks them.

Deleuze openly avows his debt to the early twentieth-century French vitalist philosopher Henri Bergson. His is, however, a 'material vitalism', for there is 'a life proper to matter', in which matter liquefies and flows. Matter indeed has the same structure as desire, which constantly outflows the boundaries of the stratified hierarchies of power. Therefore Deleuze treats the nomad as the model of all resistance to power. The drive of the state is that of 'territorialization' – to confine desire within the constellations of power, to tie it down within a specific territory. The nomad's drive is to 'deterritorialize', to cross borders, and to escape these stratifications. 'The primary determination of the nomad, in fact, is that he occupies and holds a smooth space [*espace lisse*].' But the modern capitalist world economy is also characterized by the same tendency towards deterritorialization: 'The world becomes again a smooth space (sea, air, atmosphere)'.[46]

This smooth space is that of Empire. Hardt and Negri explicitly acknowledge their debt to *Mille plateaux*.[47] More generally, Negri draws on Deleuze's vitalism to provide his version of Marxism with the philosophical underpinnings that it previously lacked. But this is at a high price, since what Deleuze offers is a highly speculative form of metaphysics. Negri's later writings thus reveal what Daniel Bensaïd has called a 'strange mysticism without transcendence'.[48]

Empire maintains the theoretical categories of Negri's version of Marxism, even if their content has changed. The social worker, for example, which in the 1970s Negri conceived as a result of what he would now call 'the disciplinary society', of the state regulation characteristic of Keynesian welfare capitalism, has become a product of the new 'informational capitalism': 'Today, in the phase of the worker militancy that corresponds to the post-Fordist, informational regimes of production, there arises the figure of the *social worker*.'[49] But Hardt and Negri prefer on the whole to use the Spinozan concept of the multitude when they seek to analyse the contradictions of Empire.

Here, where capital is genuinely global, it meets (as Rosa Luxemburg predicted) its limit. Under Empire 'the powers of labor are infused by the powers of science, communication, and language', and 'life is what infuses and dominates all production'. Social activity as such is now the source of the economic surplus: 'Exploitation is the expropriation of co-operation and the nullification of the meanings of linguistic production.' Empire is a parasitic social formation, a form of corruption that lacks any positive reality compared to 'the fundamental productivity of being' that is expressed in the multitude.[50]

Once again, we see Negri reinterpreting Marxist concepts in looser, more metaphorical terms that permit their infusion with Deleuze's metaphysics. Thus Hardt and Negri seek to bring out the negative and parasitic character of Empire as follows: 'When the action of Empire is effective, this is due not to its own force but to the fact that it is driven by the rebound from the resistance of the multitude against imperial power. One might say that in this sense resistance is actually prior to power.' As they acknowledge, this thesis of 'the priority of resistance to power' is derived directly from Deleuze, for which it is a consequence of the 'fundamental productivity' of life.[51] *Empire* is as much a work of applied poststructuralist philosophy as it is a piece of concrete historical analysis.

The limits of Empire

The most important reason for studying the history of past struggles is that it can help to clarify what strategy we should pursue in the present. But the main weakness of *Empire* is that it offers its readers no strategic guidance. The book concludes with three demands for 'a political programme for the global multitude' – 'global citizenship', 'a social wage and guaranteed income for all', and 'the right to reappropriation'.[52] One can discuss the merits of these demands – the first and the third are, as formulated, very vague, while the second is commonplace in contemporary left-liberal politics. Much more serious, however, is the absence of any discussion of how to develop a movement that could implement this programme.

The strategic vacuum in *Empire* is no mere failure of detail, but reflects some of Hardt and Negri's deepest assumptions. In one slightly bizarre passage they argue that 'the most radical and powerful struggles of the final years of the 20th century' – Tiananmen Square, the first Intifada, the Los Angeles rising, Chiapas, the strikes in France in 1995 and in South Korea in 1996–97 – did not share the 'recognition of a common enemy' or a 'common language of struggles'.[53] But, whatever may have been true of the other struggles, both the Zapatista rebellion and the French movement of November–December 1995 possessed the elements of a common political language, in both cases identifying the enemy as neo-liberalism. They therefore helped to forge the anti-capitalist consciousness that became visible at Seattle.

Hardt and Negri (who plainly wrote *Empire* before Seattle) comfort themselves with the following reflection:

> Perhaps the incommunicability of struggles, the lack of well structured, communicating tunnels, is in fact a strength rather than a weakness – a strength because all of the movements are immediately subversive in themselves and do not wait on any sort of external aid or extension to guarantee their effectiveness . . . the construction of Empire, and the globalisation of economic and cultural relationships, means that the virtual centre of Empire can be attacked from any point. The tactical preoccupations of the old revolutionary school are thus completely irretrievable – the only strategy available to the struggles is that of a constituent counter-power that emerges from within the Empire.[54]

Elsewhere Negri has reversed Lenin's old adage, declaring, 'the weakest link of capitalism is its strongest link'.[55] Now if this were literally the case, if contemporary capitalism were genuinely a homogeneous 'smooth space' in which power was distributed uniformly, then the idea of strategy would indeed cease to have much application. But this is plainly false. Different parts of the globe are of varying importance to capital. As long as the natural wealth of sub-Saharan Africa continues to be extracted by fair means or foul, large parts of the continent can be left to the tender mercies of the Four Horsemen of the Apocalypse. The much smaller portion of the Earth where the vast bulk of the productive wealth of capitalism is concentrated – still primarily North America, Western Europe, Japan, and a few Asian and Latin American extensions – is a different matter altogether. The processes of what Trotsky called 'uneven and combined development' continue to operate in contemporary capitalism, creating

huge concentrations of wealth and power at particular points of
the system. This unevenness requires strategic analysis and debate
in order to identify the enemy's points of vulnerability and our
principal sources of strength.

Strategic thought is also necessary in order to respond to what
Lenin called 'sharp turns in history', the sudden crises that offer
unexpected opportunities for the revolutionary movement if they
are recognized quickly. But Negri's entire view of history is
curiously abstract – the multitude eternally confronts capital
irrespective of the specific conditions, the accumulated contradictions, the subtle shifts in the balance of forces that the great
political texts of the Marxist tradition are so masterly in delineat-
ing. What is missing here is what Daniel Bensaïd calls 'strategic
reason':

> The art of decision, of the right moment, of the alternatives open to
> hope, is a strategic art of the possible. Not the dream of an abstract
> possibility, where everything that isn't impossible will be possible, but
> the art of a possibility determined by the concrete situation: each
> situation being singular, the instant of the decision is always relative to
> this situation, adjusted to the goal to be achieved.[56]

This kind of strategic analysis is inseparable from the attempt to
identify the agencies of transformation. Here Hardt and Negri
have little helpful to say. It is perhaps one of the advantages of
the concept of the multitude from their point of view that it
identifies the oppressed and exploited as an anonymous, amorphous mass without any definite social location. Thus they
celebrate immigrants and refugees, proclaiming 'desertion, exodus and nomadism' as a democratic force: 'A spectre haunts the
world and it is the spectre of migration.' Through overflowing
national borders and confusing all fixed identities the multitude
constitutes a new 'earthly city' in opposition to the corrupt
imperial city.[57]

Migration is undoubtedly a social and political reality of great
contemporary importance. Talking it up, however, is hardly much
of a novelty in the contemporary left-liberal academy, where for
the past decade or so multiculturalism, hybridity, and nomadism
have been deities assiduously worshipped by professorial pseudo-
radicals such as Gayatri Spivak and Homi Bhabha (both of whom
are approvingly cited by Hardt and Negri[58]). This is not the only

point where *Empire* runs the risk of breathing new life into postmodernist orthodoxy at a moment when it is showing all the signs of senile decay.

Negri wrote in 1981, 'Proletarian memory is only the memory of past estrangement . . . communist transition is the absence of memory.'[59] One can see why he should say this, despite his undeniable gifts as a historian of any political thought: any attempt critically to probe his past would expose how he – and autonomism in general – failed the Italian left in the 1970s. This refusal to confront this past is not so much an individual moral failing as a symptom of the inherent limitations of Negri's version of Marxism.

Autonomism, as I sought to indicate at the beginning of this article, is a living political force. There are, thankfully, no contemporary versions of the Red Brigades. But the idea of exemplary action on behalf of the masses remains influential, whether in the Black Bloc's cult of street violence or the *Tute Bianche*'s more peaceful tactics. These actions function as a substitute for mass mobilization. In analyses such as Hardt and Negri's the working class – reshaped in the transformations of the past few years but still very much a real force – is either dissolved into the amorphous multitude or denounced as a privileged labour aristocracy. The activists act in the name of one and try to bypass or confront the other.

Genoa exposed very clearly the limits of autonomist politics. On Friday 20 July 2001 the *Tute Bianche*'s direct action was attacked by large concentrations of police and stopped from reaching the Red Zone (the heavily fortified area of the old city where the G8 was meeting). Their leader, Luca Casarini, described what happened:

> We were attacked in cold blood, when our march was totally peaceful. They charged us first with tear gas and then with armoured vehicles, closing off all escape routes. On Friday afternoon all hell broke loose, and people were afraid of dying . . . when the charges with the tanks started, when we heard the first shots, we reacted by hiding behind garbage bins and throwing stones.[60]

All the special training and the body armour of the *Tute Bianche* could not match the armed power of the Italian state. Thousands of demonstrators, including sections of the revolutionary left, who had joined the *Tute Bianche*'s march found themselves reduced to passive onlookers at the battle. Before Genoa the *Tute Bianche* had announced the obsolescence of the traditional left:

> At last Zapatism gets rid of the 20th century – this is an irreversible and unnegotiable break from the imagery of the European left wing. It gets beyond every classic opposition of 20th century political tradition: reformism versus revolution, vanguard versus movement, intellectuals versus workers, seizure of power versus exodus, violence versus non-violence.[61]

After Genoa, however, a humbler Casarini warned against the revival of 1970s-style terrorism: 'I'm really terribly afraid of it. There are individuals and small groups that could be tempted to turn themselves into armed vanguards . . . This is the abyss that we might face in forthcoming months, if we don't change direction now'.[62] Casarini admitted that the *Tute Bianche* experience 'looks inadequate to face the imperial logic that is now before us', and advocated a move from 'civil disobedience' to 'social disobedience'.[63] If this involves a shift towards involvement in the working-class movement, that will be a step forward. Genoa starkly exposed a truth of classical Marxism that the *Tute Bianche* had so vaingloriously dismissed – only the mass mobilization of the organized working class can counter the concentrated power of the capitalist state. In romanticizing their own confrontations with this state, the autonomists have evaded the real task of revolutionary politics – the political conquest of the majority of the working class.

Toni Negri is still the key theorist of autonomism. We owe him solidarity as a victim of the Italian state. We may also respect his persistence as a revolutionary intellectual over the past four decades. But the fact remains that the influence of his ideas is an obstacle to the development of a successful movement against the global capitalism whose structures he seeks to plot in *Empire*.

Notes

1. This article originated as a talk at the Marxism 2001 event in July. I am grateful to Chris Bambery, Sebastian Budgen and Chris Harman for their help in providing material for it.

2. For example, Naomi Klein, 'Reclaiming the Commons', *New Left Review* 2:9, May–June 2001 p. 86.

3. Naomi Klein, 'Squatters In White Overalls', *Guardian*, 8 June 2001.

4. Interview in *Il Manifesto*, 3 August 2001. See also 'From The Multitudes Of Europe, Rising Up Against The Empire And Marching On Genoa (19–20 July 2001)', 29 May 2001, www.qwerg.com/tutebianche/it.

5. There is a superb account of this period in P. Ginsborg, *A History of Contemporary Italy: Society and Politics 1943–1988*, Harmondsworth 1990. For a general history of the upturn, see C. Harman, *The Fire Last Time*, London 1988.

6. For a very sharp analysis of the failure of the Italian left in this period, see T. Abse, 'Judging the PCI', *New Left Review*, 1:153, September–October 1985.

7. Ibid., p. 25.

8. *A History of Contemporary Italy*, pp. 320–32.

9. See C. Harman, 'The Crisis of the European Revolutionary Left', *International Socialism* 4, Spring 1979.

10. *A History of Contemporary Italy*, p. 382.

11. A collection of contemporary documents largely sympathetic to the movement will be found in Red Notes (eds), *Italy 1977–1978: Living with an Earthquake*, London 1978.

12. 'Judging the PCI', p. 30.

13. There is a useful study of his writing in this period in S. Wright, 'Negri's Class Analysis: Italian Autonomist Theory in the Seventies', *Reconstruction* 8 (1996). Negri had previously been a leading member of *Potere Operaio*, which organized along Leninist lines. A majority of its members joined the emerging autonomist movements.

14. See, for example, M. Tronti, 'Workers and Capital', in Conference of Socialist Economists, *The Labour Process and Class Strategies*, London 1976.

15. Quoted in 'Negri's Class Analysis'.

16. 'Judging the PCI', p. 30.

17. Quoted in J. Fuller, 'The New "Workerism" – the Politics of the Italian Autonomists', *International Socialism* 8, Spring 1980.

18. For a clear account of the difference between exploitation and the oppression suffered by, for example, the unemployed, see E. O. Wright, 'The Class Analysis of Poverty', in *Interrogating Inequality*, London 1994.

19. Antonio Negri, *Marx Beyond Marx*, South Hadley, MA, 1984, p. 173.

20. 'Judging the PCI', p. 35.

21. Negri returned to Italy in 1997 to serve out his sentence, which he was doing under fairly relaxed conditions. He was allowed to live in his flat in Rome but subject to a curfew between 7pm and 7am.

22. J. Fleming, 'Editor's preface', in *Marx Beyond Marx*, p. vii.

23. *Marx Beyond Marx*, pp. 19, 56, 94.

24. Ibid., pp. 100–101.

25. Ibid., pp. 138, 140.

26. Ibid., pp. 27, 25.

27. Ibid., p. 188.

28. Ibid., p. xvi.

29. Ibid., p. 172.

30. Ibid., p. xvi.

31. Ibid., p. 14.

32. See M. Foucault, *Discipline and Punish*, London 1977, and M. Foucault, *Power/Knowledge*, Brighton 1980.

33. Quoted in 'Negri's Class Analysis'.
34. T. Cliff, 'The Balance of Class Forces in Recent Years', *International Socialism* 6, Autumn 1979.
35. Quoted in 'Negri's Class Analysis'.
36. Spinoza, *Ethics*, in *Works of Spinoza*, vol. II, New York 1955, Appendix I, p. 78.
37. This argument is developed much further in A. Callinicos, *Is There a Future for Marxism?*, London 1982, which was written in response to the 'crisis of Marxism' of which Negri's writings of the 1970s were a symptom.
38. See, for critiques of what Robert Brenner calls 'supply-side' theories of crisis, C. Harman, *Explaining the Crisis*, London 1984, pp. 123–6, and R. Brenner, 'Uneven Development and the Long Downturn', *New Left Review* 1:229, May–June 1998.
39. See A. Callinicos, *Making History*, Cambridge 1987.
40. *Marx Beyond Marxism*, pp. 56–7.
41. See Michael Hardt, 'Translator's Foreword' in Antonio Negri, *The Savage Anomaly*, Minneapolis 1991. Negri derives the idea of the multitude from Spinoza's political writings, where it plays a much more ambivalent role than Negri is willing to acknowledge. See E. Balibar, *Spinoza and Politics*, London 1998.
42. Antonio Negri, *Le Pouvoir constituant*, Paris 1997, pp. 429, 435.
43. Ibid., p. 401.
44. Ibid., pp. 37, 40. In invoking Foucault's *History of Sexuality*, Negri ignores the very significant differences between the first volume, which appeared in 1976, and the second and third, published shortly before their author's death in 1984.
45. Deleuze's *Foucault*, Paris 1986, which Negri cites in support of his interpretation of Foucault, is in fact a rewriting of Foucault's thought on the basis of Deleuze's own distinctive ontology of life and desire. For a critical discussion of Deleuze and Foucault's treatments of resistance, see A. Callinicos, *Against Postmodernism*, Cambridge 1989, pp. 80–87.
46. G. Deleuze and F. Guattari, *Mille plateaux*, Paris 1980, pp. 512, 510, 583. Deleuze and Guattari develop a highly complex theory of the social and psychic dimensions of territorialization and deterritorialization in the first volume of *Capitalisme et schizophrénie: L'Anti-Œdipe*, Paris 1972. Deleuze is also the author of an important study of Spinoza, *Spinoza et le problème de l'expression*, Paris 1968, that heavily influenced Negri's own treatment of the same philosopher in *The Savage Anomaly*. For anti-Hegelian Marxists Spinoza tends to act as an alternative reference point to Hegel. This tendency, already evident in Althusser, is taken to its extreme by his pupil Pierre Macherey in *Hegel ou Spinoza?* (Paris 1979). Though by no means an Althusserian, Negri is consistently hostile to both Hegel and the dialectic, an attitude he shares also with Deleuze and Foucault.
47. Michael Hardt and Antonio Negri, *Empire*, Cambridge MA: Harvard University Press, p. 423, n. 23.
48. D. Bensaïd, *Résistances*, Paris 2001, p. 212.
49. *Empire*, p. 409.
50. Ibid., pp. 364, 365, 385, 387. See ibid., chs 4.1 and 4.2.
51. Ibid., pp. 360, 469, n. 13. Compare G. Deleuze, op. cit. pp. 95, 98.
52. *Empire*, pp. 400–406.

53. Ibid., pp. 54, 56, 57.
54. Ibid., pp. 58–9.
55. Title of paper delivered (*in absentia*) at the conference 'Towards a Politics of Truth: The Retrieval of Lenin', Kulturwissenschaftliches Institut NRW, Essen, 3 February 2001.
56. D. Bensaïd, *Les Irreductibles*, Paris 2001, p. 20.
57. *Empire*, pp. 212, 213, 396. The reference is to St Augustine's two cities, divine and earthly. This is one of a number of passages where Hardt and Negri draw analogies between the contemporary multitude and early or egalitarian versions of Christianity. *Empire* concludes by offering St Francis of Assisi as a model for 'the future life of communist militancy'. Ibid., p. 413.
58. Ibid., pp. 422, n. 17, 143–5.
59. Quoted in S. Wright, 'Negri's Class Analysis'.
60. Interview in *La Repubblica*, 3 August 2001.
61. 'Why Are White Overalls Slandered by People Who Call Themselves Anarchists?', 8 July 2001, www.italy.indymedia.org.
62. Interview in *La Repubblica*, 3 August 2001.
63. Interview in *Il Manifesto*, 3 August 2001.

Grass-Roots Globalism

Tom Mertes

Chaotic, dispersive, unknowable – Michael Hardt's uncertainty in the face of the multilingual mass of global oppositionists – 'a sea of people' – thronging to Porto Alegre for the World Social Forum last spring is entirely understandable.[1] There were anywhere between fifty thousand and eighty thousand participants, and at least ten thousand official delegates – activists, students, intellectuals, trade unionists, environmentalists, rural workers, Argentinian *piqueteros*, plus the representatives of scores of NGOs – crowding into seminars, round-table sessions and workshops, or marching through the sweltering streets in celebratory parades or ad-hoc protest demonstrations. Twenty-seven conferences on broad socio-economic themes were running simultaneously, together with over a hundred seminars on more specific questions – food sovereignty, 'the illusion of development', the World Bank and IMF, indigenous peoples and sustainability – and more than five hundred specialist workshops; not to mention the music, the films, the plays.

The first question, in Hardt's view, is how such a widely differentiated mass can begin to work together – for the various movements 'cannot simply connect to each other as they are, but must rather be transformed through the encounter by a sort of mutual adequation . . . not to become the same, or even to unite, but to link together in an expanding network'. The second is to distinguish the major issues they confront. For Hardt, the opponents of neo-liberal globalization are faced with a choice between two primary positions: 'either one can work to reinforce the sovereignty of nation-states as a defensive barrier against the control of foreign and global capital, or one can strive towards a non-national alternative to the present form of globalization that is equally global'.[2] Hardt and Negri have already made a passionate case against the first position in the pages of *Empire*. The modern state – born as a counter-revolutionary, absolutist response to Renaissance humanism, boosted with the toxic ideology of an exclusionary, homogenizing nationalism – has always been a tool for repression, even when posing as the champion of anti-colonial liberation. Over the past two decades, however, the powers of this reactionary instrument have been drained away by the flow of global networks of production and exchange across its borders, while sovereignty is reconstituted at the higher level of a (still somewhat misty) 'Empire'. The authors resolutely refuse any nostalgia for the power structures that preceded the global age. Strategies of local resistance – dreams of liberated zones, outside Empire – 'misidentify and thus mask the enemy', just as they obscure the potential for liberation within it. The national-sovereignty defence against the forces of international capital, Hardt now suggests, presents 'an obstacle' to global democracy.[3]

But it was this position, he claims, that dominated the official platforms and plenary sessions at Porto Alegre, promoted above all by the officials of the Brazilian PT and by the *chevènementist* leaders of the French ATTAC. The other side – the 'democratic-globalization' viewpoint – was represented by the North Atlantic anti-WTO networks, by the more radical base of ATTAC groups and, emblematically, by the Argentinian neighbourhood committees that have sprung up in response to their country's financial collapse. Hardt describes these last as antagonistic to all proposals of national sovereignty, their slogan – *que se vayan todos* – calling for the abolition of the whole political class. To further illustrate the gulf between the two positions he suggests that, if a 'democratic-globalization' solution to the Argentinian crisis exists, it would reject any national defiance of the IMF in favour of seeking 'a continuity' between the practical experiments in democracy going on at *barrio* level – the *villa miseria* in Argentina – and the democratization of the global system.

Is he right? There were certainly plenty of *memento mori* at Porto Alegre in the form of Euro-Socialist politicians looking for photo opportunities; but most of these are ardent proponents of the neo-liberal cause. Similarly, in the run-up to the Brazilian elections the PT leadership – which certainly hijacked a number of the sessions at Porto Alegre, but did not succeed in controlling its agenda – has been notable not so much for demanding sovereign control over capital flows as for its alacrity in complying with IMF demands on debt repayment. But the experience presented by activists at Porto Alegre – especially those from Latin America, where the neo-liberal crisis is at its most intense – proposed a more modulated view of the specific units and gradations of power than Hardt's 'all or nothing' approach. Rather than an intuitive uprising of the multitude against Empire, they suggested a more differentiated field.

The nation-state, precisely because of its role in pushing through the social engineering required by neo-liberalism, remains an essential instrument for global capital – and hence a key zone of contestation. It is against their own governments that both South Africans and Latin Americans have been mobilizing to fight against water and electricity privatizations. Peruvians successfully resisted an electricity sell-off – this time at local-state level, in Arequipa – earlier this year; Bolivian 'water wars' rattled Banzer's regime in April 2000; 'Vivendi, go home!' is the cry in Argentina. CONAIE, the national confederation of indigenous peoples, brought down the Ecuadorian government early in 2000, and after broken promises from the military and the new regime were back on the streets a year later to oppose austerity measures, deforestation, privatization of electricity and oil pipelines. There have been protests along similar lines in El Salvador, India, Nigeria, Ghana, Papua New Guinea. Last spring, the shantytowns of Caracas rallied to the defence of Chávez in order to fight US-backed plans for the privatization of their oil and the still greater reduction of their living standards.

'The first question of political philosophy today', write Hardt and Negri, 'is not if or even why there will be resistance and rebellion, but rather how to determine the enemy against which to rebel'.[4] The Latin American mobilizations of the past few years display not a faith in the transcendent power of national sovereignty but, precisely, a grasp of the immediate enemy – and, often, a clear intuition of the forces that stand behind him. The architecture alone of most Third World US embassies – those massive, reinforced blocks that loom more ominously than any national government buildings – not to mention the plain facts of the local USAF military base, is evidence enough. It is a common enough contradiction today that a willingness to pursue 'the radiant horizons of capitalist wealth' can sit quite easily with a sour dose of home-grown cynicism about the uses of Yanqui power.

This is the great ambivalence at the heart of *Empire*. What is the role – the 'privileged position' – of the US within the coming global sovereign power that Hardt and Negri depict? The actually existing United States constantly threatens to emerge from the pages of *Empire* like the face in a nightmare, and has to be perpetually repressed. Instructed that Empire exercises its control by means of 'the bomb, money and ether', we are warned that 'it might appear as though the reins of these mechanisms were held by the United States . . . as if the US were the new Rome, or a cluster of new Romes: Washington (the bomb), New York (money), and Los Angeles (ether).' But any such certainty is immediately withdrawn: the screen goes fuzzy – world power is much too 'flexible' for us to think of territorializing it in this way.[5] 'Empire', we are continually assured, 'has no Rome' – despite the fact that US defence spending is more than that of the next twenty-five governments combined. It has bases in at least fifty-nine countries.[6]

The US is, of course, no transcendant, deterritorialized sovereign force but only a mega-state within an international state system – as is all too clear to those who have felt its force. There are real debates to be had around questions of counter-globalization strategy at national and – more commonly proposed today – at regional level. Via Campesina's campaign for 'food sovereignty', for the right to raise protective tariffs that will prevent multinational companies wiping out local farmers by their dumping practices, is one example.[7] It is widely acknowledged that the ability of the Malaysians and the pre-WTO Chinese to impose controls on capital flow during the 1997–98 financial crisis protected their populations from much of the devastation that ravaged Indonesia. Focus on the Global South has rightly counselled Vietnam against joining the WTO, pointing out the social and economic consequences this would entail. It suggests instead 'deglobalization' to build strong regional markets within the

South that would have some autonomy from global financial interests.[8] But the traditional Chevènement position is a straw man, at least at Porto Alegre. The real questions to be asked are not about the nation-states from which sovereignty is draining away, but the one it is being sucked into.

Measures of power

For Hardt, the division at Porto Alegre between the 'national-sovereignty' and the 'democratic-globalization' positions corresponds not to Third World vs First World outlooks but to a conflict between two different forms of political organization: 'The traditional parties and centralized campaigns generally occupy the national-sovereignty pole, whereas the new movements organized in horizontal networks tend to cluster at the non-sovereignty pole.' This, he suggests, may explain why 'an old-style ideological confrontation', a clear debate between the two positions, did not take place at the 2002 WSF. Whereas the formally constituted organizations have spokespeople to represent them, the new groups do not – 'Political struggle in the age of network movements no longer works that way':

> How do you argue with a network? The movements organized within them . . . do not proceed by oppositions. One of the basic characteristics of the network form is that no two nodes face each other in contradiction; rather, they are always triangulated by a third, and then a fourth, and then by an indefinite number of others in the web . . . They displace contradictions and operate instead a kind of alchemy, or rather a sea change, the flow of the movements transforming the traditional fixed positions; networks imposing their force through a kind of irresistible undertow.[9]

One difference Hardt seems to miss is the question of scale. Many seemingly traditional bodies at Porto Alegre were actually mass organizations. The Brazilian Sem Terra is a case in point. It counts in its ranks over a third of a million landless families – and this is not a passive, card-carrying membership but one defined by taking action: risking the wrath of *latifundiários* and the state by occupying land. Within this layer there are, again, around 20,000 activists, the most energetic and committed, who have helped to organize their neighbours and who continue to attend courses and participate in regional and state-level meetings that elect the local leaderships. Over 11,000 delegates attended the MST national congress in 2000. Spokespeople – accountable to the membership – become a necessity with numbers of this size.[10] The North Atlantic networks, by contrast, are more likely to count their active core as a few dozen or less. The Ruckus Society, for example, has a full-time staff of four, and between twenty and thirty volunteers in close orbit around that; about 120 people will attend an annual camp. Other organizations like Fifty Years Is Enough and United Students Against Sweatshops (USAS) are run by less than half a dozen full-timers, who call other organizations into action. Rather than sweeping away and transforming all fixed positions, these networks often feel more at risk of being dissolved themselves into the powerful flows of American capitalism. Does size matter? For the authors of *Empire*, 'we are immersed in a system of power so deep and complex that we can no longer determine specific difference or measure'.[11] To the resounding reply of Sem Terra leader João Pedro Stedile, asked what northern sympathizers should do to help the landless farmers of Brazil – 'Overthrow your neo-liberal governments!' – their book provides no echo. Yet Stedile's demand surely suggests a scale by which the movements can take stock of their opponents, and reckon their own strength.

Hardt's maritime metaphor – the 'sea' of networks – raises a further question, crucial to the 'mutual adequation' of the current movements: waves do not speak. How, if it cannot argue but only 'sweep away' its opponents, is Hardt's network – or multitude – to hold an internal conversation, to debate and decide its strategy? For the Sem Terra, the question of how to develop democratically accountable forms of leadership and coordination, while avoiding the traps of 'presidentialism' and bureaucratization, has been literally a matter of life and death; militant farmers' leaders in Brazil have traditionally been gunned down by landowners or the state. The attempt to answer it has led them to stress the importance of collection, elected bodies at all levels, from the village occupation committee up.[12] As a result, enormous efforts are put into gathering together the far-flung activists, most of them working farmers, for regional, state and national decision-making meetings.

For North American pressure groups, radical NGOs and networks, while there is often a strong commitment to transparency
and to rotating leadership, a different sort of process often
prevails. Often these are run by a small group of dedicated
individuals who tend to lead by default, by dint of their accumulated skills. 'Obviously', as the director of the Ruckus Society puts
it, 'those closest to the centre get more input than people who
are further away from it. For example, I took the decision to hold
the WTO camp [in Seattle in 1999], and that's how a lot of the
decisions have been made since.'[13] USAS also embraces consensus
building in decision-making, with all of its pitfalls; it has only one
annual meeting of its university affiliates. With their relatively
small numbers and higher education level, the North American
groups have focused on the quality of consensus-making around
specific actions. David Graeber has described the patient and
ingenious methods – spokescouncils, affinity groups, faciliation
tools, breakouts, fishbowls, blocking concerns, vibe-watchers and
so on – that have been developed to devise summit-protest tactics,
for instance.[14] But it is not clear how these could be extended to
cope with strategic issues, or projected onto the vast scale of Porto
Alegre, where the star system – as much that of the new movements as of the traditional parties – posed another set of problems
for internal democracy.

Given these disparities, should we welcome Hardt's project of
an ever-expanding network as the form that the 'movement of
movements' should take? It seems more useful to conceptualize
the relation between the various groups as an ongoing series of
alliances and coalitions, whose convergences remain contingent.
Genuine solidarity can only be built up through a process of
testing and questioning, through a real overlap of affinities and
interests. The Turtles and Teamsters will no doubt meet again on
the streets of North America, but this does not mean they are in
the sort of constant communication that a network implies. The
WSF provides a venue in which churches and anarchists, punks
and farmers, trade unionists and greens can explore issues of
common concern, without having to create a new web.

North–South adequation

Focusing on questions of national sovereignty and organization, Hardt neglects other areas where there is perhaps a greater need for 'adequation', in some form. If – in the age of Malaysian skyscrapers and New York slums – the distinction between North and South has more to do with power and elite lifestyle than geographical location, it still denotes a significant split in current experience and historical perception. One obvious difference for activists is that the repressive nature of capitalist state power is posed much more starkly in the South. In Argentina at least 30 protestors have been killed since March 2001. At least fourteen Sem Terra activists have been murdered and hundreds jailed. Since January 2001 four protestors have been killed in the Ecuadorian Amazon and at least twenty-five shot and wounded in the highlands. In El Salvador, the death squads are back at work. In June 2001 four Papuans were killed by the state during protests against austerity measures and privatizations.[15] Genoa notwithstanding, Northerners stand a better chance of getting home safely after a demonstration.

In the end, divergences over the economy and the environment may prove more crucial than the left's organizational forms. The 'green production' laws for which North Atlantic groups have campaigned have, in practice, often worked as a form of protectionism, favouring Northern capital – and labour – while increasing poverty and unemployment in the South. Walden Bello and others have spoken passionately of the need to redress this, calling for a visionary strategy that would protect the jobs of Northern workers at the same time as strengthening the rest of the world's working class – forging a common front against the re-stratification of labour that global capital is currently trying to push through. In place of 'green protectionism', they have called for a positive transfer of green technology to the South, coupled with support for indigenous environmental groups.[16] Significantly, few of the big Northern trade unions were present to hear this case put at Porto Alegre.

Agriculture, of course, remains far more labour-intensive in the South, where a just redistribution of land is still the central issue. The threat of GM terminator seeds menaces the livelihood of hundreds of millions of small farmers across Africa, Asia and

Latin America. *Pace* Hardt's strictures on national-sovereign solutions, African governments that have refused to accept the poisoned gift of Monsanto's unmilled, self-sterilizing corn have for once been acting in the interests of their citizens. Via Campesina – itself a North–South alliance of working farmers – held its own mini-forum at Porto Alegre, in a park near the city centre; Monsanto and Coca-Cola logos were ritually burnt at its closing ceremony. First World environmentalists need to listen attentively to these Third World farmers and indigenous groups, who unite powerful ecological concerns with a highly critical perspective on international capital.

A third division – here, no longer on North–South lines – was over the question of global capitalism itself. While almost all the speakers and participants were critical of the IMF, World Bank and WTO, there was disagreement over whether these institutions could be reformed, or whether they were inherently linked to a system that is fundamentally unequal, corrupt and unsustainable. For all the attention paid to these general issues, however, there was far less debate on the current world political situation. When the questions on which any global oppositon might be expected to raise its voice were discussed – the US war in Afghanistan, the Middle East, the threat to Iraq – it was often away from the central plenaries and official platforms, though such issues did surface after the initial presentations.

The debate over the WSF needs to remember, too, the exhausting logistical problems that global organizing presents to the dispossessed. Time, money and a daunting sense of distance present real obstacles to students, activists, trade unionists, the rural and urban poor – in stark contrast to the well-funded global infrastructures of the ruling class. For all his reservations about the Brazilian PT, Hardt must acknowledge that without its municipal government in Porto Alegre, the WSF would never have taken place. Naturally, most of the participants were from Latin America – Brazil, Argentina and Uruguay between them fielded over 7,000 delegates, Italy and France around 1,200. Travel problems percluded many more. The hard-working interpreters – translating into Portuguese, the host language, and English, although Spanish might have been a more natural *lingua franca* for most of those present – often went unpaid for their skills.

Organizing from below is a fragile process, at threat from

numerous different forces. A micro example: when LA-based activists recently sought to get in touch with *maquiladora* workers in Mexico, they first had to negotiate their way through a series of blocking attempts by the moderate NGOs that controlled the funds for transport and translators, and wanted to run the agenda too. When finally the Angelenos met with their Tijuana counterparts, they found that what the *maquiladoristas* needed most was computers – to send information out but, above all, to get news in. The US side could come up with the computers; what they couldn't produce was electricity, decent phone lines, Spanish-language software and technical help.

Hard as it is, this sort of grass-roots organizing remains crucial for building up relationships of mutual support, coalitions of resistance. In these nano-level processes of forging solidarity the WSF – and especially perhaps its informal side: the youth camp, fiestas, lunches, marches – can play a vital role. 'Chaotic, dispersive, unknowable' as they may be, these messy, mass-scale face-to-face encounters are the life-blood of any movement – an element that telecommunications metaphors can never attain.

Notes

1. See 'Today's Bandung?', *New Left Review*, no. 14, March–April 2002.

2. Ibid., p. 114.

3. Michael Hardt and Antonio Negri, *Empire*, Cambridge, MA, 2000, pp. 83, 103, 133, 307, 43–6; 'Today's Bandung?', p. 117.

4. *Empire*, p. 211.

5. Although, on the very next page – the decline of the nation-state notwithstanding – we find a cool analysis of the 'imperial' tasks – 'the construction of information highways, the control of the equilibria of the stock exchange despite the wild fluctuation of speculation, the firm maintenance of monetary values, public investment in the military-industrial system to help transform the mode of production, the reform of the educational system to adapt to these new productive networks, and so forth' – that currently demand 'big government' in the USA.

6. Center for Defense Information, *World Military Database 2001–2002*, http://www.cdi.org/products/almanaco102.pdf.

7. See interview with José Bové, 'A Farmers' International?', *New Left Review*, no. 12, November–December 2001, pp. 94–5. While *Empire* famously promotes the subversive effects of mass migration, Hardt and Negri also defend, more poignantly perhaps, the right of the 'multitude' to refuse to move. In this instance, a strategy for Asian and African farmers – some third of the world's workforce – to defend their livelihood through some form of regional counter-sovereignty becomes imperative.

8. Walden Bello, 'Pacific Panopticon', *New Left Review*, no. 16, July–August 2002, pp. 77–9.

9. 'Today's Bandung?', pp. 115–7.

10. See interview with João Pedro Stedile: 'Landless Battalions', *New Left Review*, no. 15, May–June 2002, p. 85.

11. *Empire*, p. 211.

12. 'Landless Battalions', pp. 85–6.

13. John Sellers, 'Raising a Ruckus', *New Left Review*, no. 10, July–August 2001, p. 75.

14. 'For a New Anarchism', *New Left Review*, no. 13, January–February 2002, pp. 71–2.

15. For further details of numbers of protestors killed – many fighting IMF austerity measures – see *States of Unrest II* (2002) at http://www.wdm.org.uk/cambriefs/Debt/Unrest2.pdf.

16. 'Pacific Panopticon', p. 80.

Notes on Contributors

Gopal Balakrishnan is Harper-Schmidt Assistant Professor at the University of Chicago, and a member of the *New Left Review* editorial board. He is the author of *The Enemy: an Intellectual Portrait of Carl Schmitt*, and editor of *Mapping the Nation*.

Michael Rustin is Professor of Sociology and Dean of Faculty of Social Sciences at the University of East London. He is the author of *The Good Society and the Inner World* and *Reason and Unreason: Psychoanalysis, Science and Politics*.

Stanley Aronowitz is Professor of Sociology at CUNY graduate center. He is the author of *The Knowledge Factory* and *From the Ashes of the Old: American Labor and America's Future*.

Charles Tilly is Professor of Social Sciences at Columbia University. He is the author of *Democracy and Contention in Europe, 1650–2000*, and *Durable Inequality*.

Giovanni Arrighi is Professor of Sociology at Johns Hopkins University. He is the author of *The Long Twentieth Century*.

Sanjay Seth teaches Political Theory at La Trobe University, Melbourne, Australia. He is the author of *Marxist Theory and Nationalist Politics: The Case of Colonial India*.

Leo Panitch is Professor of Political Science at York University. He is the author of *Renewing Socialism: Democracy, Strategy and Imagination* and editor of *The New Imperial Challenge*.

Sam Gindin is Assistant to the President of the Canadian Auto Workers Union.

Ellen Meiksins Wood is Editor of the *Monthly Review*, and formerly Professor of Political Science at York University, Toronto. She is the author of *The Origin of Capitalism* and, most recently, *Empire of Capital*.

Malcolm Bull is a Fellow of St. Edmunds Hall, Oxford, and a member of the *New Left Review* editorial board. He is the author of *Seeing Things Hidden: Apocalypse, Vision and Totality*.

Timothy Brennan is Professor of English at the University of Minnesota, Minneapolis. He is the author of *At Home in the World: Cosmopolitanism Now* and *Salman Rushdie and the Third World: Myths of the Nation*.

Alex Callinicos is Professor of politics at Derwent College, University of York, and a member of the editorial board of International Socialism. He is the author of *Against Postmodernism: a Marxist Critique*.

Tom Mertes is Administrative analyst of the Center for Social Theory and Comparative History, UCLA, and a member of the *New Left Review* editorial board.

Acknowledgements

Chapter 1: *New Political Economy*, vol. 7, no. 1, March 2002.

Chapter 2: *The Nation*, July 17, 2000.

Chapter 3: *Canadian Journal of Political Science*, xxx, 1, 2002.

Chapter 4: *Historical Materialism*, vol. 10, no. 3, 2002.

Chapter 5: *Third World Quarterly*, 23:3, 2002.

Chapter 6: *Historical Materialism*, vol. 10, no. 2, 2002.

Chapter 8: *London Review of Books*, October 4, 2001.

Chapter 9: *Critical Inquiry*, vol. 29, no. 2, winter 2002.

Chapter 10: *International Socialism*, 92, autumn 2001.

Chapter 11: *New Left Review* 17, September–October 2002.

Index